YALE ORIENTAL SERIES

RESEARCHES

VOLUME XVIII

AMS PRESS

NEW YORK

YALE ORIENTAL SERIES · RESEARCHES · VOLUME XVIII

PSEUDO-EZEKIEL
AND THE ORIGINAL PROPHECY

BY

CHARLES CUTLER TORREY

Professor of Semitic Languages
in Yale University

NEW HAVEN
YALE UNIVERSITY PRESS
LONDON · HUMPHREY MILFORD · OXFORD UNIVERSITY PRESS
MDCCCCXXX

Library of Congress Cataloging in Publication Data

Torrey, Charles Cutler, 1863–1956.
  Pseudo-Ezekiel and the original prophecy.

  Reprint of the 1930 ed. published by Yale University
Press, New Haven, which was issued as v. 18 of Yale
Oriental series: Researches.
  Bibliography: p.
  Includes index.
  1. Bible. O.T. Ezekiel—Criticism, interpretation,
etc.   I. Title.   II. Series: Yale Oriental series:
Researches; v. 18.
[BS1545.T6   1980]   224'.406   78-63562
ISBN 0-404-60288-6

International Standard Book Number
Complete Set: 0-404-60270-3
Volume 18:   0-404-60288-6

MANUFACTURED
IN THE UNITED STATES OF AMERICA

PREFACE

The Book of Ezekiel, as it has stood before the world for more than two thousand years, affords the most remarkable single illustration of the triumph of the Hebrew Chronicler's ingenious and picturesque, but utterly impossible, history of the Jewish church in the Persian period. Here is a prophecy originally composed in Jerusalem, and from beginning to end addressed to the people of Jerusalem and Judea, which has been made over in a perfectly transparent manner into a product of the Chronicler's 'Babylonian exile.'

The original character of the book is as clear as daylight; the wonder is, that it should have remained so long unrecognized. The internal evidence is unequivocal, and as complete as such evidence could possibly be. The basis upon which the author built his elaborate work was the brief characterization of the wicked reign of Manasseh given in 2 Kings 21: 1–17. This, and the subsequent history contained in the Book of Kings (Kings only, not Chronicles), gave the writer all of his material which deals directly with the Jewish people.

The prophecy in its original form is seen at once to be a very late production; the evidence as to this is many sided and in the aggregate overwhelming. It is the latest of all the canonical Old Testament prophecies with the exception of the second half of Daniel.

To those scholars—and they are a multitude—who are unwilling to believe that the canonical Hebrew-Jewish literature includes pseudepigrapha, but maintain that all the documents of our Old Testament, from Deuteronomy to Ecclesiastes, were written at the various dates and by the various authors named in them, this demonstration will present little of interest. To those, on the other hand, who believe that the employment of the historical imagination by Hebrew religious teachers could be legitimate and useful I would submit that no period in the whole history of Israel could offer an opportunity of religious instruction comparable to the one here utilized. The Ezekiel in Jerusalem warned and called to repentance those who were on the brink of destruction; the seer of 'Tell Abib' was only beating the air.

The interpretation here presented does not bring into view a new prophecy, it merely renders an old prophecy for the first time comprehensible. The weight of a long tradition is very great, and deservedly

5

so, especially in the case of writings of such supreme importance as the
Hebrew scriptures. I know, and am glad to know, that this new picture
of the prophet will be met with suspicion. I believe, however, that in
the end it will be recognized as the only interpretation which satisfies
the evidence, literary, historical, and I may even add traditional, for I
shall show that the ancient Jewish scholars knew with what they were
dealing.

C. C. T.

New Haven, Connecticut,
January 1, 1930

LITERATURE

The following is a list of the principal works to which especial reference is made in the present volume. Herrmann's *Ezechiel* contains a very nearly exhaustive catalogue of the modern literature dealing with this prophet and his book.

Smend, *Der Prophet Ezechiel.* 1880.

Bertholet, *Das Buch Hesekiel.* 1897.

Kraetzschmar, *Das Buch Ezechiel.* 1900.

Herrmann, *Ezechiel.* 1924.

Hölscher, *Hesekiel.* 1924. (Beiheft 39 zur Z.A.T.W.)

Rothstein, in Kautzsch's *Heilige Schrift des A.T.*, 4te Auflage, Vol. I. 1922.

Cornill, *Das Buch des Propheten Ezechiel.* 1886.

Toy, *The Book of the Prophet Ezekiel.* Critical Edition of the Hebrew Text. 1899. A new English Translation. 1899.

Selle, *De Aramaismis libri Ezechielis.* Diss., Halle, 1890.

Dürr, *Ezechiels Vision von der Erscheinung Gottes (Ez. Cap. 1 u. 10) im Lichte der vorderasiatischen Altertumskunde.* 1917.

Burrows, *The Literary Relations of Ezekiel.* Diss., Yale, 1925.

Also, the commentaries on Jeremiah by Duhm, Giesebrecht, and Cornill.

CONTENTS

I

THE JEWISH TRADITION

The temporary rejection of Ezekiel by some of the Jewish scholars who undertook to form a 'canon' of sacred scripture is a very remarkable fact. From what knowledge we possess as to the manner of this general undertaking, we should say that the selection of the 'canonical' writings was carefully made in accordance with a liberal policy. The religious value of each writing considered was of course a prime requisite. There was also a chronological requirement, putting the lower limit in the latter part of the Persian period; the apparent intention having originally been to include whatever important religious writings suitable for public use could fairly be claimed to antedate the Samaritan schism.[1] Prophecy, according to the accepted view, had been extinct since the time of Nehemiah or a little later; see especially Josephus, *Contra Apionem*, I, 8.[2] Only writings which were the fruit of divine inspiration (that is, in every case, inspiration given to *a prophet*) could be used in the service of the synagogue; and this public use as sacred scripture is what 'canonicity' practically signified. Even such valuable works as the Proverbs of Ben Sira, 1 Maccabees, and the Wisdom of Solomon could not be admitted to the sacred library. On the other hand, the work of the Chronicler, Proverbs, Koheleth, Song of Songs, Daniel, and Esther (not to mention others) could be admitted, the decision in their favor turning undoubtedly upon the fact that they could be given—and actually were given—an early date. In the case of a few of these, as is well known, there was outspoken opposition maintaining that the writing in question was not inspired scripture, that it did not "defile the hands." In other cases, objection to the public use of the book was made on other grounds. As far as the single criterion of date is concerned, there is evidence that the difficulty of late origin had been overcome for various writings in various ways, as early as the third century B. C., and even here and there by a process of re-

---

[1] See my *Second Isaiah*, pp. 96–98.

[2] Josephus, to be sure, assigns the work of Nehemiah to the reign of Xerxes, and makes Esther the last canonical book, dating it in the time of Artaxerxes I; in contrast with the older (massoretic) chronology, according to which Nehemiah flourished under Artaxerxes II.

11

touching which might have seemed to some the restoration of the original text; thus, in the case of Habakkuk one or two very slight alterations (הכשׂדים instead of הכתים, 1:6, and היין instead of היוני, 2:5) sufficed to give the little masterpiece a setting in the time of Nebuchadrezzar instead of that of Alexander the Great. The well-meaning gloss, "This was Zerubbabel" (1 Esdras, 4:13) secured for the interpolated Story of the Three Guardsmen a temporary place in the Chronicler's great history, until the critical decision of the Jewish authorities at Jerusalem removed it, at the beginning of the second century of the present era.

The hesitation in regard to Ezekiel was unlike that felt in the case of any other book. No one, as far as we know, ever openly maintained that it was not, or did not contain, sacred scripture. The Jewish reader heard in it the voice of a true prophet, whose message was divinely inspired and whose written book unquestionably would "defile the hands." Yet the question was debated, whether it could be admitted to the public use of the synagogue, that is, made formally *canonical*.

The most obvious reasons for including the book of Ezekiel in the inner circle may be enumerated here. 1. Its own claim to be the utterance of a divinely inspired prophet is persistent and emphatic. "Son of man, go and speak unto the house of Israel"; "All my words that I shall speak unto thee receive in thy heart"; "Thou shalt say unto them, thus saith the Lord God; and they, whether they hear the message or disregard it, yet shall know that there has been a prophet among them"; "I have made thee a watchman unto the house of Israel; therefore hear the word at my mouth, and give them warning from me"; "And they shall know that I am the Lord"; "Then I spoke all the things that the Lord had showed me." Such words as these are to be found on every page of the book. In no other portion of the Old Testament, not even in the latest stratum of the book of Jeremiah, is the claim to be a divine message repeated so often and with such emphasis.—2. The early date of the book is made equally plain. It is dated over and over again, by year, month, and day, in a way that only the work of the Chronicler can parallel. Here is a prophecy older than Haggai, Zechariah, Malachi, and Daniel; a voice from the time when the God of Israel still spoke directly to one of his people, entrusting him with a public mission.—3. In its religious content, the prophecy of Ezekiel deserves a high place among the Hebrew writings. It is a most impressive utterance, startling in its denunciation, earnest in its warning, and inspiring in its promise. It is no mere repetition of what others had said, but makes its own weighty contribution to Hebrew theology. It is a carefully planned and self-consistent whole, with some strikingly eloquent passages, both prose and poetry. It seems, moreover, to throw light upon a chapter of Hebrew history concerning which the Chronicler is our only other source of information.—4. The prophet, according to the belief current at the time when the canon was fixed, and indeed for several centuries previously, was one who was given a vision of future events. That which distinguished him from every ordinary preacher of righteousness, that which especially gave him his credentials, was his ability to announce beforehand what should take place. Every one of the prophets of Israel was believed to make his definite prediction, which the subsequent course of history eventually justified. The Jewish public was entitled to hear of every clear manifestation of this divinely given power.

Now the book of Ezekiel contains some very wonderful examples of such prescience. Along with these there are other predictions which, while decidedly impressive, could hardly be called wonderful. In chapters 4–7 the prophet foretells the siege of Jerusalem, the extremity of famine in the city, its ultimate capture, the profanation of the temple by foreign invaders, the slaughter of some of the people and the scattering of others into foreign lands, where they will dwell in distress and humiliation; the destruction of the 'high places' which crown every hill and mountain in the land, and the affliction of all Palestine. In this, with all its surprising fulfilment in detail, there is perhaps nothing exceeding the possibility of mere human foresight. In chapters 34–37 the restoration of Jerusalem and the holy land is predicted. This will be effected by the return of the scattered children of Israel "from all the nations and countries" in which they have been dwelling.[3] This promise, however, might have been uttered by any Hebrew prophet after the seventh century B. C.; that is, after the beginning of the great dispersion.

---

[3] It is quite noticeable that in the many and varied occurrences of this prediction there is never mention of Babylonia as one of the lands from which the people are to return.

The proofs of miraculous vision are ample, however; and in their startling definiteness they are paralleled only by those found in the Book of Daniel. For example, the seer knows, through his divine gift, that Nebuchadrezzar is to lay siege to Jerusalem in the ninth year of Zedekiah, in the tenth month, on the tenth day of the month (24:1 f.). He foretells a long siege, and grievous famine in the city (4:16); the flight of Zedekiah by night (12:12) with a band of his followers, making a breach in the wall of the city (*ibid.*); the capture of the king and the dispersion of his guard (vs. 13 f.); the judgment at Riblah (11:9 f.); the blinding of the king, and his captivity in Babylon (12:13). Now we know from 2 Kings 25:1-7 that precisely these things took place when Jerusalem fell, in the year 586. According to the exact and consecutive dates given in the book, the foregoing predictions were made well in advance of the events; those relating to Zedekiah in or before 591, and that concerning the arrival of Nebuchadrezzar in January, 588. No more striking evidence of prophetic foreknowledge (like that of Daniel) could possibly be given. There are numerous other astonishing predictions, clearly beyond the range of mere human foresight, which need not be mentioned here, as they will receive notice in the sequel.

When all this is considered in connection with the other features of the book, described above, we certainly may say that to all appearance no prophet of Israel had, or could have, stronger attestation than this one. In any question of 'scripture profitable for instruction'—such instruction as in fact has been afforded by 'Ezekiel' in synagogue and church for nearly two thousand years—we should suppose that this ancient prophecy would make an irresistible claim. Nevertheless the book was for a time refused admission to the inner circle. It is the purpose of the present chapter to show that the hesitation on the part of the Jewish scholars was more deeply significant than has been realized in modern times.

I believe that the real cause of the temporary rejection has long been hidden from sight and is at present unsuspected. I also believe that the learned authorities in Jerusalem in the first century of the present era showed their practical wisdom in that they did not give out to the public the true reason for the objection which had been felt; but instead fixed attention upon other and less important matters, in such a manner as to put an effective barrier in the way of any of their people who might incline to a "higher criticism" of the book.

The Talmud gives one definite reason for the hesitation over Ezekiel. The familiar passage, occurring in more than one place (*Shabbath* 14 b, *Chagiga* 13 a, *Menachoth* 45 a), tells how, when the book was in danger of being "withdrawn" (גנז) "because its words conflicted with those of the Torah," it was restored by Hananiah ben Hezekiah. "What did he do? They brought him 300 jars of oil and he sat in an upper chamber and explained it." The "picturesque story" (Moore, *Judaism*, I, 246) is quoted as a tradition which was well known.

Now this is good-humored camouflage, nothing else. No one of the learned men of the time when it originated can possibly have regarded it in any other way. The enumeration of the "300 jars of oil" was made with a twinkle in the eye, and so also was the statement regarding the conflict of Ezekiel's words with those of the Torah. The Pentateuch was quite able to stand on its own feet. The Law of Moses, which had been followed for many centuries and was incomparably sacred, was in no danger. The Jewish scholars, who were past masters of interpretation, could have felt no difficulty in allowing these fanciful predictions to hold their own place. Even the unskilled interpreter was relieved of any trouble by one very significant feature of the prophet's prescription. *When* were these new regulations to go into effect? The "ordinances of the altar" (that most singular construction) were appointed for "the time when it shall be made" (43:18). This was also the time when the (strikingly artificial) "allotment of the land for inheritance" should be accomplished (45:1). When *could* any such division be made? Had the leaders of the Jewish people any reason to feel present concern about this utopia? It is all ideal, and in the perfectly indefinite future. "From that day on, the name of the city shall be *Yahwè-shammah*" (48:35); but for the present, and presumably for the rest of the present age, the city would continue to be called Jerusalem. If, as would seem likely, the prophet is speaking of the Messianic time, which he more than once expressly predicts (as in 34:23 ff. and 37:24 ff.), *that day* and the Mosaic law could be left to take care of themselves. Was Ezekiel a prophet, with a divine message? If so, no human being could presume to criticize or set aside, while there existed no difficulty whatever in interpreting the message.

Did any one besides Hananiah ben Hezekiah ever read the details of his vindication of Ezekiel? We do not know. Certainly they were not important enough to be preserved. In *Menachoth* 45 a the various points of disagreement between the prophet and the Pentateuch are mentioned and discussed, but by no means with any citation of Hananiah. On the contrary it is said, repeatedly, that when Elijah comes these matters will be finally explained. It would not require 300 jars of oil to say this much; and we should have been led by the story to suppose that even Elijah was not necessary. The motive of the story, obviously, was to provide a reason for the official decision (which could not be forgotten) putting an end to controversy over the book and admitting it to 'canonicity.' The real cause of the controversy was hidden, and that of necessity, under a mere pretext.

It was not merely with the closing chapters of the book that the Jewish authorities had difficulty. Jerome, in his much-quoted Epistle to Paulinus, doubtless informs us of a custom of long standing when he says that accórding to the Jewish regulation (*apud Hebraeos*) the beginning and end of Ezekiel are to be read only by those who have reached thirty years of age. That is, the youthful critic is warned to keep his hands off these portions of the prophecy. Why, now, the warning against *the beginning* of the book? We see that the 'conflict with the Pentateuch' was not the only source of trouble, perhaps not even the chief source. I think it will become increasingly evident that the danger seen by those who put forth this interdict was located in the opening verses of the first chapter. It was not desirable to say this, and the anecdote of the 300 jars of oil gave sufficient reason for including the last chapters in the warning.

The reason eventually given for the interdict against the first chapter was that it gave rise to theosophical speculations (see Moore, *Judaism*, I, 300). This it undoubtedly would do, and such speculation was undesirable; and yet it was hardly such a bugbear as this prohibition would make it. It is not likely that the picturesque imagery of the first chapter of Ezekiel has ever led any one into serious error. Literary imagination, symbolism, allegory—these had already become commonplaces even to the youth under thirty years of age. There was material for speculation in the Book of Daniel, and in other scriptures. Moreover, that dangerous celestial vehicle, the *Merkaba*, is not presented in the first chapter only. It appears again, in full detail of description, in chapter 10; yet the warning was never given, nor intended, against *the first ten chapters* of the book! It is plain that something more troublesome than the *Merkaba* lay behind the original prohibition, in spite of the later interpretation. We must look further.

The true reason for warning the immature student, and for the temporary regulation that *the first chapter* of Ezekiel should not be read in the synagogue (Moore, *ibid.*) is one which could not possibly be given, for in giving it the mischief would be done. The indefinite "Hands off!" was the most that could be said. The student is instructed to accept the judgment of his elders without undertaking to construct theories of his own; and there was a most important reason for this advice. Before the reader of Ezekiel has fairly begun the first chapter he is face to face with a *crux* of the very first magnitude, one in fact on which the fate of the whole book depends. In its presence theosophical speculations and conflicts with the Torah sink into absolute insignificance.

The prophecy has two beginnings, mutually exclusive. After the prophet has begun to speak in the first person, telling of a vision which came to him and giving its date, his narrative is interrupted by an insertion which introduces him in the *third* person and with a *different* date. The first date, in vs. 1, is "the thirtieth year." This, according to the custom of dating where no particular era or epoch is mentioned, would be supposed to mean the thirtieth year of the reign in which the prophecy was uttered (and, as eventually will be seen, this is precisely what it does mean). According to vs. 2, the initial vision was seen "in the fifth year of the captivity of King Jehoiachin." This belongs to a system of dating which extends through the whole book, forming a series which, while perfectly self-consistent, has given great trouble to commentators. This system of dating is closely connected—indeed, inseparably connected—with the location of the prophet and the bulk of his prophecy in Babylonia, in a community of Jewish exiles, "the Golah," which is represented as including the main body (or all) of those who had been carried away from Jerusalem into captivity, so that it could be addressed as "the house of Israel." Herein is still another obvious difficulty, for there is no part of the long prophecy, forty-eight chapters, which if no setting were assigned to it would naturally seem to be addressed to exiles in Babylonia or elsewhere, while on the contrary large portions of it are obviously and expressly addressed to the people of Jerusalem and Judea.

What might a prophet speaking to "the Golah" be expected to say? Certainly something, however brief, that would apply definitely and specifically to them in their experience, their present condition, and their hope for the future. Since there is no message of the sort, not even a single paragraph that would not apply equally well, or much better, to Jews living in perfect freedom in the land of their fathers; while on the other hand the only prophecies whose hearers can be located by the content of the admonition addressed to them are in Judea; does not the contradiction seen in the opening sentences of the book give ground for a strong suspicion? The youthful Jewish student in the first century of the present era, if he were unhampered by any restriction laid upon him by his elders, might very easily have got thus far. He undoubtedly, moreover, would have given to the existing learned tradition of his own people as to the authorship of the book greater weight than our modern scholars are willing to give. Before considering this last point, however, it will be well to print the opening passage in a way to indicate to the eye the lines of cleavage that would appear to one who was inquiring. There is a problem here which neither scholar nor prophet could reduce to minor significance. In the startling directness with which it stares every reader in the face, with no interval to lessen the shock and no ground for suspecting accidental re-shaping of the text, it stands alone among the puzzles of the Old Testament.

Now it came to pass in the thirtieth year, in the fourth month, in the fifth day of the month, **as I was among the** captives by the river Chebar, *that the heavens were opened, and I saw visions of God.* **In the fifth day of the month, which was the fifth year of King Jehoiachin's captivity, the word of the Lord came unto Ezekiel the priest, the son of Buzi, in the land of the Chaldeans by the river Chebar; and the hand of the Lord was there upon him.** *And I looked, and behold, a stormy wind came out of the north,* etc.

This certainly looks like *editing*; the later introduction of a new scene and a new date, while leaving the old date untouched. The technique of adapting a document, with the use of editorial additions and slight alterations, must have been perfectly familiar to any young Jewish scholar worthy of the name. Here is the obvious necessity of a critical analysis of the first verses of the book, recognizing an older stratum and a later expansion. Ancient and modern readers alike have seen this. It remains to be seen what bearing the fact has on the main questions of the character, authorship, and date of the prophecy. Before dismissing the subject for the present it may be useful to quote the words of Kraetzschmar, *Das Buch Ezechiel* (Nowack's Handkommentar), p. 1: "Sphinxgleich an der Schwelle dieses an Problemen und Schwierigkeiten überreichen Buches lagernd geben gleich die drei ersten Verse dem Leser Rätsel auf, an deren Lösung Generationen schon vergeblich sich abgemüht haben." And after enumerating the difficulties presented by the three verses he adds: "Alle Versuche, diese Anstösse hinwegzudeuten, sind gänzlich unbefriedigend." True; but a Jewish higher critic of the first century would have solved the riddle offhand, if he had been given a clear field. There was information still available which would have confirmed his suspicions.

What, now, is the old Jewish tradition, the earliest at least of which we have knowledge? What did the learned men of Jerusalem, seriously undertaking to answer questions as to the actual genesis of the several books of the Hebrew Bible, have to say in regard to the book of Ezekiel? Nothing whatever as to its origin in Babylonia. They seem on the contrary to have been quite clear in their opinion that the book which we have was *not* written in Babylonia. They manifest, moreover, a most significant skepticism as to the authorship of the entire prophecy. The well known passage in *Baba Bathra* 14 b and 15 a contains food for thought, not least in the portion dealing with the Prophets. Isaiah is recognized as composite, while assigned as a whole to the time of King Hezekiah. "Jeremiah wrote his book"; but *"The men of the Great Synagogue* wrote Ezekiel, the Twelve Prophets, Daniel, and Esther." As for the Twelve Prophets, it is of course partly the redaction of the 'book' that is intended, and that in fact did take place somewhere near the middle of the third century B. C.; some statement that would apply to all the Twelve was obviously necessary.[4] It is likely that in

---

[4] Modern scholars see little or nothing worthy of credence in the legend of the 'Great Synagogue.' It is true that what is actually reported as to its membership and its share in the history of Judaism is merely fantastic, but it may well be that the legend is based

this collocation there was also the design of leaving open the questions of date and authorship, even while appearing to settle them. Who could now be sure what was meant by the words: "the men. . . . *wrote*"? Daniel and Esther are here assigned to their true relative position in the literary history; the prophet Daniel was not a member of the Great Synagogue, and his book was composed after his generation had passed away.

The pronouncement as to Ezekiel, however, is not merely unexpected, it is truly startling. The commentators have been at a loss to explain it. The query of Wildeboer, *Entstehung des alttest. Kanons*, is repeated by Bertholet, *Comm.*, p. XXIII: "Sollte darin noch eine Reminiscenz an die Entstehungsgeschichte unseres Buches liegen?" Obviously, seeing that the whole passage is dealing solely with Entstehungsgeschichte. Nevertheless it has not been customary to take these words of the Talmud at their face value. For the supposition that a *redaction* of the prophecy is intended, there is no warrant in the book itself; nor has any plausible reason ever been suggested why the prophet whose name it bears should not have been pronounced its author. It is a very markedly uniform and monochrome composition, as the great majority of interpreters have seen and said. The same peculiar style and diction appear in every chapter, the flavor of the poetry is exactly that of the prose. As to the essential coherence of the book, Smend's judgment, supported by a very careful and thorough analysis (pp. XXI ff.) is well known: 'The entire book is the logical development of a series of ideas according to a well considered plan. . . . . Observe the strict logical connection and progress in the several divisions of the work. . . . . This renders it extremely probable that the whole book was written at one time (in einem Zuge).' Bertholet, from his own independent literary study, shows how the entire composition is symmetrically disposed, with the successive parts in a logical sequence which is quite unmistakable. See pp. XIX f. and XXIII. No redaction could possibly have produced such a result, nor has any re-

---

on a genuine tradition. In my *Second Isaiah*, in the chapter dealing with the formation of a Sacred Library (pp. 94–101), I showed the necessity of supposing the existence in Jerusalem, in the third century B. C., of an authoritative body of scholars who collected and edited the writings attributed to the 'Later Prophets.' May not the tradition of the Great Synagogue have preserved a reminiscence of this body?

dactor disturbed the general plan. Some commentators, in despair of fitting certain portions of the book to the setting in Babylonia and the 6th century, have attempted an arbitrary analysis, but with no result which can survive critical examination.

"Wrote," in the passage in *Baba Bathra*, cannot mean "collected and edited." The history of exegesis sufficiently demonstrates that the book of Ezekiel does not ordinarily make the impression of embodying the continuous compositions of two or more writers. On the contrary, certain strongly marked literary characteristics run through the whole work, from the first chapter to the last. Certainly this fact was not unperceived by the Jewish readers. The essential self-consistency, the progress in thought, so evident to modern scholars, must have been still more clearly discerned—or else taken for granted—by the learned men in Jerusalem. Nothing even remotely approaching this homogeneity and definiteness of plan is to be seen in Isaiah or Jeremiah. Yet "Jeremiah wrote his book." We have indeed seen that there is in Ezekiel the appearance of an editorial insertion at the beginning, and other brief additions by the same hand will eventually be pointed out; but the great prophecy still belongs to the prophet. The presence of an external touch of this nature, or of a series of such embellishments, cannot deprive the author of his manifest right. It must not be forgotten that the whole prophecy is given *in the first person!* Did any prophet ever have a clearer title to 'his book' than Ezekiel?

Why, then, did the authorities in charge of the Jewish tradition refuse to say that "Ezekiel wrote his book"? The obvious reason is the only possible reason: Simply because *they knew that the book was not written by the 'Ezekiel' of the Babylonian captivity.* If, as I believe I shall be able to show, and as all the many-sided evidence seems plainly to indicate, the original prophecy was composed about the year 230 B. C., while the 'exilic' editing was accomplished still later, it is in every way probable that the main facts of the origin of the book would have been preserved in learned circles in Jerusalem and known to some of those who were confronted with the question of its canonicity. This, and only this, could account for the opposition which the book received, and for the "camouflage" (as I have felt justified in terming it) under which it was finally admitted to the collection of the Hebrew Prophets.

Beyond all question there were some to whom the initial date, "in the thirtieth year," presented no riddle. The familiar custom of dating joined to the material content of the prophecy would have made the matter as clear as daylight to a critical scholar of the second century B. C., for date and content agree in the most complete and striking manner. Facts were then in the foreground which later became obscured. The *second* date would at the same time have been seen by him to be impossible, an unwarranted interpolation; or rather, the first of a formidable series of interpolations. Moreover, since along with his acquaintance with customs of dating he must certainly have possessed some knowledge of the Neo-Babylonian reigns, he would not need to be told that "in the thirtieth year," *without any further definition, could not possibly have anything to do with Jewish exiles in Babylonia. Here was a book of prophecy which was seriously, all but fatally, damaged by a false mask which plainly did not fit. What was to be done with it? If it had not been a work of extraordinary interest, it doubtless would have shared the fate of the vast majority of Hebrew writings, religious as well as secular. But the claims of the prophecy, especially those set forth in the early part of this chapter, could not be gainsaid; it must by all means be given a place in the sacred library, and thus be saved for the public use.

The one great obstacle in the way of the adoption was the telltale contradiction in date and setting, and this could not be removed. It was not a case for a single surgical operation, like that which the authorities in Jerusalem performed when they cut out the intolerable Story of the Three Youths from the book of Ezra (*Ezra Studies*, pp. 57–59; *A.J.S.L.*, XXXVII, 1921, p. 91). Here, the insertions belonging to the spurious redaction are not only scattered through many chapters, but also are uncertain in extent and in the manner of their combination with the original text. The analysis is bound to be more or less arbitrary. An investigator of the twentieth century may have the audacity to undertake this precarious task, but in Jerusalem 1900 years ago any such attempt would have been unthinkable. It is no wonder that there was at first serious opposition to the 'canonization' of Ezekiel. Of course the most conspicuous source of trouble could have been removed once for all by the simple (even though dangerous) expedient of excising from the first verse of the first chapter the words "in the thirtieth year." But *this was the original date*, the one prefixed by the prophet himself, and even the thought of destroying it would be impious.

The only hope of saving the great prophecy for perpetual use lay in the course wisely adopted: to take the book as it stood, and issue a warning to critics. The only way of calling off such investigators from the seat of danger without actually pointing it out was to devise a warning which, while including it, should divert attention from it. This was admirably done, by putting the danger-sign on both ends of the book, with the chief emphasis on the closing chapters. Hence the anxiety about the Torah, and the rescue of the prophecy with the aid of 300 jars of oil. But when there was need to answer the direct question, *Who wrote the book?* the reply was ready, and was handed down faithfully. The oldest Jewish tradition tells its own plain story. It recognizes no Babylonian prophet Ezekiel.

II

THE PROPHET'S HEARERS AND "THE GOLAH"

It is necessary at the outset to discuss a question of fundamental importance, one which has never been satisfactorily answered: To what hearers was the prophecy addressed? "To the exiles in Babylonia, of course," will be the reply of some who never have read the book carefully. More attentive readers will agree that the bulk of the prophecy, aside from the oracles predicting the fate of foreign nations, is directly addressed to the people of Judah and Jerusalem. How extensive, precisely, is this "bulk"? The prophet's appointment to his mission is most impressive. He is sent with a message of dire calamity and a call to repentance to "a rebellious house," to "the house of Israel," to the "children of Israel." This would naturally be supposed to mean the Hebrews of Palestine; not merely because of the long-standing use of these terms, but also because any assemblage of 'exiles' who could be addressed by an 'exilic' prophet would be a very small fraction of the Israelite people. It is certain that the prophet is given no formal message definitely applied to Jews living in Babylonia; it remains to be seen whether his prophecy, or any part of it, can be supposed to have reached such an audience.

In the first chapters of the book, at least, there is no ambiguity as to the content of the divine oracle of rebuke and warning. *"Son of man, I send thee to the children of Israel,* to peoples that are rebellious, which have rebelled against me; they and their fathers have transgressed against me, even unto this very day. And the children are impudent and stiffhearted. I hereby send thee unto them; and thou shalt say to them, thus saith the Lord God. And they, whether they will hear, or whether they will forbear (for they are a rebellious house), yet shall know that there hath been a prophet among them.....*And thou shalt speak my words unto them,* whether they will hear, or whether they will forbear; for they are most rebellious." And again (3:4-10): "Son of man, go, get thee unto the house of Israel, and speak my words unto them. For thou art not sent to a people of strange speech and of a hard language, but to the house of Israel; not to many peoples, whose

24

words thou canst not understand; surely, if I sent thee to them, they would hearken unto thee. But the house of Israel will not hearken unto thee, for they will not hearken unto me; for all the house of Israel are of a hard forehead and of a stiff heart. Behold, I have made thy face hard against their faces, and thy forehead hard against their foreheads. ....All my words that I shall speak unto thee receive in thine heart, and hear with thine ears." Verses 17–21 set forth in startling terms the duty of the prophet to deliver such a warning as shall turn sinners from their sin, and save them from the approaching calamity, showing them plainly God's purpose, and the doom which is impending because of their unexampled wickedness. *"Son of man, I have made thee a watchman unto the house of Israel; therefore hear the word at my mouth, and give them warning from me.* When I say unto the wicked, Thou shalt surely die; and thou givest him not warning, nor speakest to warn the wicked from his wicked way, to save his life; this wicked man shall die in his iniquity, but his blood I will require at thine hand. Yet if thou warn the wicked, and he turn not from his wickedness, he shall die in his iniquity; but thou hast delivered thy soul."

This means, unquestionably, that the message is to be delivered *in person* to those for whom it is intended. The prophet is sent on a desperate errand. "All the house of Israel" (3:7) is arrayed against him, in open apostasy and insolent self-confidence.[5] He must face them courageously, speaking in the name of the Lord. His warning will save some from the doom which will overtake the rest.

The actual message, for which the way has thus been prepared, appears at length in chapters 4–7. It is addressed only to Jerusalem, the mountains of Israel, and the holy land. It predicts the capture of the city, after the horrors of famine and pestilence which attend a long siege; the destruction of the heathen sanctuaries at all the high places; slaughter in the city and throughout the land; and the scattering of

---

[5] It can hardly escape notice, how ill this characterization fits any Hebrew community *after* the descent of the Chaldeans upon Jerusalem, the siege and capture of the city, and the deportation at the end of Jehoiachin's reign. Such phrases as those in 5:7; 7:11, 24b; 23:42, and the arrogant words of the leaders of the people of Jerusalem in 11:2 f., are not what would be expected. (I believe that in 11:3 instead of the reading בְּנוֹת בָּתִּים the original was נְכוֹת הָעִיר, and that after the infinitive had been accidentally miswritten the noun "houses" was substituted *ad sensum*.)

the people of Israel among all the countries. This is expressly said to be because of the wickedness in Jerusalem and "all the evil abominations of the house of Israel" (6:11) in the holy land. The long address of accusation and warning which the prophet is commanded to deliver is spoken directly, in the second person, to these evil-doers. Thus 7:7, "Thy doom is come upon thee, O inhabitant of the land; the time is come, the day is near; disaster, not imaginings" (read *harhōrīm*, comparing Dan. 4:2. Not a word is said about sinners in Babylonia. We therefore seem to know with certainty to what hearers the prophet was sent, when he received his divine appointment.

In the chapters which follow, the situation is not different. Chap. 10 is occupied with the theophany, a repetition of chap. 1; chaps. 17 and 19 contain parables depicting the sin and punishment of Judah and Jerusalem such as might have been uttered anywhere; chaps. 25–32, 35, and 38 f. are oracles against foreign nations; every other portion, from chap. 8 to the end of the first "book," i.e. to the end of chap. 39, deals solely with the Hebrews of Palestine, almost everywhere in the form of direct address.

Against these patent facts the current interpretation of Ezekiel stands out in singular incongruity. According to this theory, set forth in all modern commentaries, the Babylonian exiles were a wicked and arrogant community. They are rebels and "scorpions" (2:5 f.); the prophet must expect personal violence from them (Kraetzschmar on 2:6, pp. 25 f.). His mission, nevertheless, is to "go to them of the captivity and speak to them," to "be to them a reprover," to "warn the wicked from his wicked way," to tell his neighbors (for he is of the Golah): "Thus saith the Lord; whether they will hear, or whether they will forbear" (3:11, 15, 26 f.). In spite of their wickedness they were very strongly attached to Jerusalem and the temple. Ezekiel accordingly prefers not to speak to them of their own sin, but instead proclaims to them, from day to day, the guilt of "the bloody city," "the rebellious house of Israel," "the defiled sanctuary," the renegade prophets, priests, and princes in Judea (22:24–28), the holy land filled with abominations; and announces the speedy coming of a terrific catastrophe upon southern Palestine, involving the destruction of Jerusalem. His preaching was at first unheeded, and his claim to have divine authority was mocked at by the exiles; so the commentators must and do assert (see e.g. Smend, XVII, XIX, and Bertholet on 3:22). The men of the Golah refused to believe that Jerusalem was in any danger (they seemingly had completely forgotten the recent siege and capture of the city and the subsequent deportation by the Chaldeans). Ezekiel is forced to produce his credentials. He accordingly foretells exactly the disaster of the year 586, writing down for his incredulous neighbors the date, to a day, on which the siege of Jerusalem is to begin, and describing just those details of the capture and destruction of the city, and the fate of Zedekiah and his people, which are narrated in 2 Kings 25 (Ezekiel, chaps. 12 and 24). Some time after this (33:21 f.) a fugitive comes to Tell Abib and confirms all that the prophet had foretold. The exiles hear the tidings with horror and consternation; they are thrown into utter despair ("schwärzeste Hoffnungslosigkeit"). Undoubtedly they now recognize that a prophet "has been"[6] among them. Whether the wicked community of Tell Abib thereupon became less wicked, we are not given ground for surmising. The prophet continues with a long message of comfort, addressed to the Israelites who are now "scattered among the nations and dispersed through the countries" (36:19, and elsewhere). This is repeated through several chapters, but with no mention of Babylonia, nor with any word of either comfort or exhortation which could apply specifically to that land or to his supposed neighbors.

The glaring fact in regard to the prophetic ministry thus depicted is its utter futility. The prophet has not been faithful to the charge given him by the God of Israel. He certainly has not been a watchman to the house of Israel, nor is it clear what he has been doing in the years of his service. There is indeed little appearance of reality in this picture of Ezekiel and his surroundings. There is nothing convincing, nothing self-consistent, in the tissue of conjecture regarding the Babylonian preacher and his Babylonian audience. What seems to be certain (because actually asserted in the Hebrew text) at one moment is flatly contradicted in the next. Were the deported Israelites really such em-

---

[6] As Smend (on 2:5) truly says, there is no other way of rendering the היה which regularly occurs in this formula. It certainly does not apply to the situation in Tell Abib. If, on the other hand, the prophet is delivering his message in Jerusalem, he will of course no longer be "among them" after the destruction of the city and the slaughter and scattering of its inhabitants.

bodiments of evil as are described in 2:5 f., 3:7–9, 19; 14:3; and if they were, why did not Ezekiel venture to rebuke and warn them? Certain it is that in these passages he is said to dwell among such miscreants (also 12:2, and elsewhere), and equally certain that when we suppose him to be addressing them he is in fact speaking to the inhabitants of Jerusalem.

The customary depiction of 'the exiles' as profoundly stirred, and with salutary result, by the final demonstration of Ezekiel's divine authority is pure assumption, and without guarantee that the assumption is well founded. In such a situation as that commonly supposed for Ezekiel it is indeed quite conceivable that a great company of former citizens of Jerusalem should be moved by an impassioned portrayal of the guilt, and the impending doom, of the city and land from which they had come. This could by no means be taken for granted, however. Much would depend on the moral and religious condition of these hearers, and the nature of their customary outlook into the future. It is also conceivable—and far more likely—that they would hear the invective with apathy (if they listened to it at all), or else with a certain bitter satisfaction in the prediction of dire punishment. As Bertholet remarks (p. XIII), they had "nicht viel Grund, auf die Zurückgebliebenen sonderlich gut zu sprechen zu sein." If they were an obdurate, irreligious community, they certainly would not care a straw for the preacher's fulminations against the land which they had left behind once for all. His warnings, addressed either to those who were too far away ever to hear about them or else to those who were under no necessity of heeding them, would have fallen perfectly flat.

Even the 'convincing proof' by fulfilled prediction decided nothing for those who were not inclined to be convinced. The claim of supreme power for Yahwè the God of Israel, accompanied by striking evidence, was no new thing to the 'people of the Golah.' They had heard it from their childhood, and with some acceptance; otherwise they would not have been so deeply attached to the temple in Jerusalem, and so confident of the divine power which preserved it, as the current theory represents them. The news of its destruction, so far from increasing their faith in Yahwè, would have been much more likely to cause them to doubt his existence, or at all events his supremacy. Ezekiel had indeed foretold these things "in the name of the Lord," but his power to look into the future might come from another source than that which he claimed. If our modern commentators can persuade themselves (as they frequently do) that Ezekiel foresaw the various happenings as a clairvoyant while in an ecstatic condition, without any help from the God of Israel, it is not difficult to suppose that the stubborn-hearted exiles at Tell Abib could have reached a somewhat similar conclusion. "Gods many and lords many" were recognized by Ezekiel's immediate hearers (14:3–7, for example), and any one of a multitude of daemonic agencies might have given the seer his information.

If, nevertheless, we accept without reserve the assumption that Ezekiel's hearers were convinced by his demonstration of foreknowledge and satisfied as to his credentials, the fact remains that to all appearance the demonstration was made for the sake of Ezekiel himself, rather than for that of his congregation in Tell Abib. They shall know that a prophet has been among them; but they have not been his chief interest, nor does his subsequent preaching concern them directly. His face is saved, and a discomfiting "I told you so" is now in order; but this little triumph is neither the fruit of a divine message nor the reward of a true prophet. Have we not in some way been misled as to the scene and immediate objective of this seemingly impassioned prophecy?

The all-important fact, frequently stated with emphasis in the preceding pages, is that the prophet's formal call was to speak to the people of Judah and Jerusalem, and that his recorded discourses are actually addressed to them. The spectacle of a religious teacher launching his invective and warning, day after day and year after year, against sinners who are far distant and incapable of receiving any profit from his exhortation is decidedly unpleasant. Hence Smend, in his final appraisal of the book and its author (p. XVI), says that Ezekiel at Tell Abib was not, and could not be, a prophet; the prophet must have an audience worthy of his message and to which he can speak directly. Ezekiel, addressing the people of Jerusalem, can only imagine them as within hearing distance, or by some artifice pretend to bring the city before his eyes (künstlich vergegenwärtigen). In the light of these well considered words let the reader review the prophet's own conception of his great commission, as set forth in 3:17–21 (see above). He is bidden to warn the children of Israel, the inhabitants of

the holy land, who without his aid are doomed soon to perish in their
wickedness. If their blood is not to be required at his hands, if he would
save his own soul, he must tell them what is in store for them, and why,
and deliver to them the promise of the God of their fathers to save
every man who will repent. With this tremendous responsibility laid
upon him, what he proceeds to do is to draw pictures on a tile and
declaim to the men of Jerusalem who are many hundreds of miles distant from him, unable either to see his symbolic tile or ever to know
what he has said! This, if the prophet is indeed in Babylonia, is much
more than folly, it is wretched mockery. Kraetzschmar, p. V, while
admitting the strangeness of Ezekiel's manner of obeying the divine
command, would justify him by suggesting that although he had within
his reach only a fraction of his countrymen, yet he "regarded his
mission as directed to the whole people" (da er seine Mission doch stets
als an das gesamte Volk gerichtet angesehen hat). This, in effect, is an
attempt to save the prophet's faithfulness to duty by making him out
an imbecile. The recently numerous proposals to 'explain' Ezekiel as
'a pathological subject' have their important substratum of truth, but
do not touch the principal and ever present difficulty, and fall far
short of satisfying; because of the great underlying absurdity which
has not been cleared away, the obvious and total incongruity of the
prophecy with the setting assigned to it. If the prophet, the "Ekstatiker," really made no better use of his great opportunity than this which
now appears, the sooner his book is consigned to a *genizah*, the better;
we should not feel grateful to Hananiah ben Hezekiah.

Bertholet, p. XV, asks whether the 10,000 exiles among whom Ezekiel dwelt did not constitute an audience sufficient to save his reputation
as a prophet. Against this stands, in the first place, the unquestionable
fact that the prophet, after receiving his formal call to speak to "the
house of Israel," actually begins his mission by a long address, obviously
fitted to the terms of his call, in which he takes account successively
of Jerusalem, the mountains of Israel, and "the four corners of the
land" (chaps. 4–7). This certainly makes it plain that he himself conceived the recipients of his message to be living in Palestine. It is true
that in one of the verses containing his instructions the term "the
children of thy people" is given a very singular definition (3:11): "Go,
get thee **to them of the captivity** unto the children of thy people, and

speak unto them, and tell them, Thus saith the Lord; whether they will hear, or whether they will forbear." And, in accordance with this, vs. 15 narrates how Ezekiel made his way to Tell Abib and remained there seven days before beginning to utter his prophecy (which, as the commentators remark—see Kr., p. 35—would have been expected to begin without any such delay). It remains to be seen what relation these very strange interruptions, utterly out of keeping with the context in which they stand, have to the equally disturbing interpolation at the beginning of the first chapter.[7]

Another strong objection to Bertholet's attempt to avoid the contradiction lies in his assumption of a congregation of 10,000 exiles. He finds the number provided, to be sure, in 2 Kings 24:13 f.; but it is too palpable an exaggeration to be taken seriously. Jer. 52:28, in a summary which professes to give the exact numbers of each deportation, informs us that the total of those who were carried away with Jehoiachin was 3023. It is easy to decide which enumeration is the more deserving of credence. But even the smaller figure is much too large for the supposed settlement of Jewish exiles at Tell Abib.

Peaceable emigrants, or exiles, who would make for themselves a home in a strange country must go in small numbers, or disperse widely when they reach the new land, unless it happens that they are given effective aid from without. We certainly may not think of the 'exiles of Tell Abib' as a great detention camp supported and supervised at the expense of the Babylonian government, nor were they handed over to contractors for forced labor. The Chaldean captors let their captives shift for themselves, after they had removed them far from the possibility of mischief. Yet we are shown the members of this deportation, only a little more than four years after their arrival in the strange land, dwelling in a small city of their own, care-free and presumptuous, seemingly enjoying every ordinary comfort. "The exiles had their own houses and lands, and their own government by elders" (Toy, *Translation*, p. 92). From whom were these lands and houses taken? In what conceivable way could such a community, lacking every resource, have maintained itself at all, to say nothing of achieving speedy prosperity?

[7] In connection with the mention of the "seven days" at Tell Abib it may be well to call attention here to the very significant *doublet reading* in 3:16. Apparently the original text made no mention of an interval of seven days.

Some one has suggested that the Babylonian exiles probably lived on dates, which grow abundantly in Mesopotamia. Not so at Tell Abib. Ezekiel had in abundance wheat, barley, beans, lentils, millet, and spelt, and could eat by weight twenty shekels a day (4:9 f.). He had at his disposal such furnishings as a tile, an iron pan, and balances for weighing (4:1, 3; 5:1). Nowhere is there any hint of straitened circumstances, the impression given is just the contrary. According to the narrative in 2 Kings, those carried away from Jerusalem in 597 were not farmers. Even if they had been, they could not have achieved so astonishing a result in so short a time. There doubtless were artisans among them, but artisans could have found no means of support.

History has shown how nearly impossible it is, under ordinary circumstances, for large expatriated groups to subsist when left to themselves. At the time of the Hijra from Mekka, Mohammed instituted the 'Brotherhood,' in which each of the generously devoted Helpers in Medina took one or more of the fugitive Mekkans under his protection. Even so, it was some time before the latter (whose needs certainly were not great!) were able to stand on their own feet. Even thoroughly equipped and hardy colonists, scattered about in small groups, have a struggle before them. In modern times, comparatively small Jewish settlements in Palestine, given every advantage, and most generously supplied with funds and material equipment by their supporters in wealthier lands, have found the way to prosperity very slow. The great difficulty of maintaining the deportation colonies in Australia in the early years, in spite of excellent provision and expert supervision, is well known; and so also is the problem presented at the present day to philanthropists in their attempt to keep alive large companies of refugees, made homeless by the devastation of war.

When the Chaldeans, or other conquerors, deported their captives with no intention of letting them starve to death, they distributed them, a few score here, a small company there, as the only possible course of action. In this way, unquestionably, the deportation in the time of Jehoiachin was scattered. It is quite another matter when a large portion of the population of a city or town is removed, and another population installed in its place, as not infrequently was done. Thus Nisibis was transferred from the Greeks to the Persians in the year 364; and thus also a number of the Hebrew cities of the northern kingdom of

Israel seem to have been more or less completely changed in character through a process of deportation and repopulation by exchange from foreign cities. But "Tell Abib" is not a Babylonian name, and we need not query whether a Babylonian city was evacuated for the benefit of these captives. Kraetzschmar, p. 34, attempting to find an explanation for the (improbable) name of this locality, remarks that there are enormous sandhills, called *til-abubi*, scattered throughout all Babylonia; "Is it not probable," he asks, "that practical Nebuchadnezzar settled the main body of the Jews on a nameless *til-abub*, in order that they might make the sandy surface into arable land?" If this had been done, and the whole deportation had remained in that place, it might with good reason have been predicted that a visitor of a later day would find the slopes of the hill containing no living being, but only 3023 skeletons.

We may say with certainty that there can have been no extensive settlement of Jewish captives at the time and under the circumstances depicted in our present book of Ezekiel. There were, of course, considerable groups of Hebrews in Babylonia, as in Egypt, Phoenicia, Southern Arabia, Greece, and elsewhere; trading settlements which grew up gradually. These groups ultimately flourished, and made their influence powerfully felt throughout the Jewish world. But as for those inhabitants of Jerusalem and Judea who were deported to Babylonia, we have no good reason to suppose, but very strong reason to doubt, that any portion of them constituted a settlement which ever was heard from again. The author of the Books of Chronicles (and the school to which he belonged) had no difficulty in imagining, and creating, great assemblies of captives. As I have shown elsewhere, this was the all-important feature, the central fact, in the Chronicler's peculiar history.

The question now recurs, with considerably increased significance: *Where, and to what audience, were these prophecies uttered?* and the way has been prepared for giving it a final answer. The prophet was commanded to "speak," not to write; and we are told of certain groups of discourses that they actually were delivered. A few facts applying to the prophecies themselves, in distinction from what is said *about* the prophecies, are important enough to be repeated with emphasis. The

Hebrew *exiles* there mentioned are dispersed, or to be dispersed, among all the nations and countries. There is nowhere any implication that the branch of the dispersion which is (or is to be) in Babylonia has a special importance of its own, or that its members are on a different footing from those in other lands. The prophet never predicts a return of exiles from Babylonia specifically, nor expresses the hope that there may be such a return. He nowhere appears to be addressing a company of his countrymen in Babylonia, nor is there in any of his discourses even the slightest indication of a Babylonian setting.[8] It is easy to show that the scene of the original prophecy is Jerusalem, and that Palestinian hearers are presupposed in every direct address to an audience. The entire 'exilic' situation is merely a matter of editorial patches, usually attached or inserted in a very clumsy manner. A few of these patches have already received mention in the preceding pages. One of them, especially, has attracted universal attention, and moreover has generally been recognized in its true character as an interpolation; although, strangely enough, no one hitherto has understood the motive of its insertion. Rothstein, in Kautzsch's *Heilige Schrift des A. T.*[4], comments as follows on Ezek. 1:2 f.: "Hier hat eine fremde Hand in den Text eingegriffen; freilich ist nicht einzusehen, was sie dazu bewogen hat." On the contrary, the motive is as clear as daylight; it is the same which produced the great work Chronicles-Ezra-Nehemiah and led to the ill-fated Cyrus-Babylon insertions in Second Isaiah. In the editorial additions to the original Ezekiel the fiction of 'the Golah' in Babylonia is presented in its crudest form.

The terms "house of Israel," "children of thy people," etc., are frequently and plainly defined by their context, as we have seen. They always designate the Hebrews of Palestine, particularly those of the Kingdom of Judah. The frequently occurring epithet *beth meri,* "rebellious house," has the same meaning—everywhere. Notice the significant use of the verb in 5:6 (at the beginning of the prophecy) and again in 20:8; cf. also 2:3, and see Toy, *Trans.*, note on 11:17. The prophet himself dwelt in this *beth meri,* see 2:5; 3:26; 12:2; 24:3; 44:6. That is, during all the scenes and discourses of this book he is in Jerusalem,

---

[8] The words "whom ye have left behind" (very obviously interpolated) in 24:21 do not constitute an exception, for they could apply equally well (or ill) to any of the countries of the dispersion.

not in 'Tell Abib.' This is quite evident even in chap. 12, in spite of certain easily recognizable alterations of the original text which the Babylonian redaction necessitated, and which will be discussed in a later chapter of this volume. The symbolic action performed by Ezekiel is comprehensible only as intended for the eyes of the people of Jerusalem. Verses 3–6, 9 f., 15, and 20 ff. show that they in fact were the recipients of the message. Verse 19, *"And say unto the people of the land"* (!), actually declares this in so many words. No wonder that the commentators are bewildered. Bertholet writes: "Auffällig ist die Anrede an das 'Volk des Landes.' Hes. weilt ja nicht unter ihm." But the phrase is fortified by the whole chapter—to say nothing of the other chapters.

The prophet is surrounded by false prophets and prophetesses, priests, and elders. The false prophets are mentioned particularly in chaps. 13 and 22. One would not expect prophets to attract any attention among recently deported exiles, especially if their oracles concerned far distant Jerusalem (13:16). As for the prophetesses, decking themselves and going about "to hunt souls" (13:18 ff.), they seem improbable in a newly founded settlement of Jewish captives. In 22:24–28, however, it is made plain that the false prophets, like the unfaithful priests, are in Judea. Princes are mentioned in the same context (vs. 27).

Three passages mention the *elders* who were among Ezekiel's neighbors. In 8:1 they are called "the elders of Judah," and in 14:1 and 20:1 ff. "the elders of Israel." These are characterized as *idolaters*; see 14:3–7; 20:3 f., cf. vss. 16, 28 ff., 39. In chap. 8 nothing further is said concerning those particular elders who "sat before" Ezekiel until he was carried away by the spirit to the inner court of the temple. In the following vision, however, he is shown "the elders of the house of Israel" (vss. 11 f.) doing sacrifice to "all the idols of the house of Israel," and this in the temple at Jerusalem. It is natural to suppose that the elders of vs. 1 belonged to the same group as those mentioned in vss. 11 f.; otherwise, why were they introduced at all? The scene of chap. 14 is very obviously Jerusalem. The "multitude of idols" (vs. 4) is the same multitude which had been mentioned in 8:10. In his reply to the elders, the prophet addresses "the house of Israel" (vss. 5 f.); includes "the strangers that sojourn in Israel" (vs. 7); specifies then more particularly the land of Judea (cf. vs. 15 with 5:17); and finally names Jerusalem as the city whose representatives have thus inquired of the prophet (cf. vss. 7b, 8 with 21 f.). The fact that Ezekiel dwells in the city, and is inquired of, cannot save its people unless they repent. Even Noah, Job, and Daniel could not deliver the land which is doomed. The case in chap. 20 is equally clear; see especially vss. 27, 30 f., 33 f., 39. It is in Judea, not in Babylonia, that the elders come to inquire of the prophet. Any other supposition reduces impressive warning to a futile tirade. The sin of idolatrous 'elders' at Tell Abib could not be rebuked by threatenings against Jerusalem.

The prophecies of chap. 21 are even more evidently spoken in Jerusalem than are those in chaps. 20 and 22. In 21:1 (20:45) the prophet takes his stand on the heights of Jerusalem, looks toward the Negeb, and utters a parable: Fire will be kindled in a great forest. Then he turns his face back to the city (vs. 6), and speaks to the land of Israel. Thus far, there is nothing to show that he is speaking to actual hearers. But in vss. 23–28 (18–23) there is a definite statement which makes it certain that he is conceived as addressing a veritable audience, and also that this audience is in Judea, not in Babylonia. The prophet predicts here, as often elsewhere, by means of a pantomine accompanied with verbal explanation. But the witnesses and hearers of the prediction are obdurate, as usual. Yahwè himself foretells the result (vs. 28): "It will be unto them as a false divination in their sight (these who bind themselves by oaths, to violate them!).⁹" This very evidently refers to Zedekiah and his fellows; see the last clause of the verse, and the direct address to the king in vs. 30. Compare 17:13–20 (and 16:59) and also Jer. 34:10 f., 15 f. Ezekiel's pantomime was performed "*in the sight*" of these men of Jerusalem, who scoffed at it. In no other place would the action have been significant or have aroused any interest. Thus Smend: "Gemeint sein kann nur, dass Ez.s Weissagung bei den Judäern keinen Glauben findet."

The editor permitted this to stand; it could be explained away, if

---

⁹ I believe that we should read נִשְׁבָּעֵי in place of שְׁבֻעֵי, though the latter may possibly be correct (as a colloquialism). The original of להם was certainly לְהָפֵר; observe that in the ordinary Aramaic script (papyri, ostraca, etc.), in which this book undoubtedly was written and copied, the character כ is the *exact* equivalent of פּר. In any closely written text only the context can show which is intended.

the location at Tell Abib were sufficiently assured elsewhere. Not so, however, in chap. 33, the central importance of which is evident. Here, in vss. 1–9, is characteristically repeated the prophet's formal commission, the same which had been given in 3:16 b–21. He is appointed as *a watchman to the house of Israel.* The words "When I bring the sword upon a land" (vs. 2) may of course be claimed to be merely figurative; and yet compare 14:17, and see the conclusion of this chapter, vss. 27–29, 33! In vs. 10 Ezekiel is commanded to speak to the house of Israel, to those who are saying, "We are to 'pine away in our iniquities'; how then should we live?" This is a direct (scoffing) allusion to the prophet's direful prediction in 4:17 *concerning the people of Jerusalem* who are to perish by famine and pestilence after the fall of the city. Farther on, in vss. 23 ff., he is entrusted with a special message to those who "inhabit the waste places in the land of Israel." Portions of the land had been abandoned, partly because of the devastation wrought by the raiding bands in the time of Jehoiakim (2 Kings 24:2) and by the Chaldean armies in 597; even more, doubtless, because of the great Dispersion (*Ezra Studies*, pp. 293 –297). The final catastrophe is yet to come, both upon the city and upon the land (vss. 27–33), and the prophet, the 'watchman,' must warn these who are in danger, if he will deliver his own soul and not be held guilty of their blood. He is twice commanded to *speak to them* (vss. 25, 27). A prophet dwelling in Judea might easily bring the word of God to these doomed people; not so one dwelling in Babylonia! Throughout the discourses of the chapter the situation is perfectly clear: the prophet is in Judea, speaking to Judeans.

All this is so evident, the parallel with chapter 3 is so important, and the inference so obvious, that the "fremde Hand" (see above, p. 34) again undertakes a correction. In the former instance the prophet and his audience were summarily transported to Babylonia by the interpolated verse 3:15 and two words in 3:11; in the present case the same result is achieved by a surprising editorial performance. Plump into the middle of the chapter (for it is a literary unit) is thrust the curious episode of "the one who had escaped from Jerusalem," vss. 21 f. Aside from the barbarous interruption of the prophet's discourse, the details of the inserted passage are such as to arouse lively suspicion. The arrival of a single fugitive 1½ years after the fall of the city has

little verisimilitude, and the excessive brevity with which his message
is reported is not at all in the manner of the prophet. The date in vs.
21 has been objected to since the earliest times, and some ancient
versions and mss., as well as some modern commentators, have wished
to change the reading (see Theodoret's remark quoted in Field's
Hexapla). It is excellently attested, however, and in its true character
as an editorial manufacture is about what might be expected. See
also Chapter IV, on the original sequence of dates.

What effect has the message from Jerusalem upon the people who
are in Ezekiel's neighborhood? The question is not unimportant. It
does not appear that they hear the news at all; certainly they pay no
attention to it. They continue to regard the prophet as a mildly en-
tertaining creature, whose eloquence is worth hearing from time to
time, as when one listens to an expert musician (vss. 30–32).[10] It is the
same ineffective curiosity which their elders displayed in chaps. 8 and
20: "Come along, let's 'inquire' of the prophet and hear what he will
say." If the captives at Tell Abib heard the report of the destruction of
Jerusalem and the temple and the devastation of Judea, they certainly
did not take it seriously. But this is not all; the prophet himself does
not believe it! For him, *the great catastrophe*, the one which he has been
predicting from the first, *is still in the future*. Words could hardly state
this more plainly than it is stated in vss. 28 f. and 33. "I will make the
land a desolation and an astonishment, *and the pride of her power shall
cease*" (cf. 7:24 and 24:21). "Then shall they know that I am the
Lord, when I have made the land a desolation." "And when this comes
to pass (behold, it is at hand!), then shall they know that a prophet
has been among them" (cf. 7:1, 7; 21:12; 24:24). Is there in all literature a more striking example of an interpolation which is contradicted
by its context?

The superficial *modus operandi* of this editor is even more clearly
shown in his operation with the prophet's 'dumbness.' In 24:25–27 he
had prepared the way for the present interpolation. It had been re-
vealed to Ezekiel (so this appendix to the original prophecy declares)
that after the destruction of the city and the temple a fugitive would
come to Babylonia and bring him tidings of the event; thereupon 'his
mouth would be opened, and he would be dumb no longer.' (In vs.

---

[10] This interesting passage will receive notice in a subsequent chapter.

22, in place of the first *wa-yiftach* read *liftoăch*.) Accordingly, when the arrival of 'the fugitive' is narrated in 33:21 f., we are told that the prophet was again able to speak, so that the Jews at Tell Abib were given their 'sign' (24:27). This is clever, but singularly heedless and clumsy. The notion of the prophet's dumbness is taken from 3:26; where however the closing of his mouth by divine command is only for the brief period during which he is shut up in his house, engaged in performing his first symbolic action; until 'the days of his siege' are fulfilled; see 3:24-27; 4:7 f.; 5:2. From that time on (in spite of the thoughtless notion of our redactor) he is a prophet engaged in the full and unrestricted exercise of his public office. No commentators' quibble can make him out to be otherwise. To declare him 'dumb' in any sense whatever, in such chapters as 5, 11, 13 f., 20 ff., 24, 33, is preposterous.

The origin of the two related passages, 24:25ff. and 33:21 f., is quite clear. They came from the same hand which inserted verses 2 f. in the first chapter, and made other additions to the original text, all with one and the same purpose. One reason why chap. 24 was given several embellishments of this kind lies in the nature of the principal occurrence described in it, which seems to require Jerusalem as its scene. In case of the ordinary discourses and depictions it is possible for the reader to persuade himself (if he feels obliged to) that the seer transfers himself in imagination from Babylonia to Palestine. The sticking point comes when the seer performs a symbolic action in the sight of his neighbors. Here the reader can hardly avoid recognizing a real occurrence and a real scene. In two of the chapters, 12 and 24, the scene is so evidently Jerusalem that the editor must make alterations of some sort, if the fiction of the 'exilic prophet' is to be maintained.

There was the same necessity, similarly met, in other places. In chaps. 8-11 the prophet is in Jerusalem and in the temple, unmistakably represented as seeing actual occurrences, whether natural or supernatural (10:2, last clause), not things merely imagined. How explain this? The original prophecy had represented the seer as carried by the spirit from one place to another (3:12-14; 8:3, 7, 14, 16; 11:1; 40:2 b, and numerous passages in chaps. 40 ff.), and the same mode of transportation is now adopted by the editor for the greater distance. The spirit lifts the seer by the hair of his head, and carries him back and forth between Tell Abib and Jerusalem, in the same way that Habakkuk, somewhat later, is carried to Babylon for Daniel's benefit. The statement of transfer is made in the fewest possible words—see 8:3 (a small part of the verse) and 11:24 f.—and is employed only where it is absolutely necessary. Thus, in 8:1 the prophet is *in his own house*, while in vs. 3 b and thereafter he is in Jerusalem; it must therefore be established at once that his home is not in this city, but in Chaldea. So also again, in chap. 12, from the first verses onward, we are shown the prophet in his own home; and the symbolic action described is so obviously suited to Jerusalem only, that without definite statement that it was performed among the 'captives' it would carry with it the very similar pantomimes in chaps. 4, 5, 21, and 24. Hence, of necessity, the verses 11:24 f. This is an ingenious conception, sufficiently effective until suspicion is aroused and the startling incongruities are inquired into. But this drastic device for insuring an 'exilic' prophecy gives way when it is tested; it puts too great a strain on the prophet's hair.

In chap. 11 there is a very remarkable passage, to which commentators have hardly done justice. Ezekiel, speaking at Tell Abib, foretells in eloquent language and startling terms the doom which is impending over the holy city and all its inhabitants. As he utters his terrifying prophecy, Pelatiah the son of Benaiah, who is in Jerusalem (vs. 1), falls dead. At this, the prophet cries out in anguish. Vs. 13: "And it came to pass, when I prophesied, that Pelatiah the son of Benaiah died. Then fell I down upon my face, and cried with a loud voice and said, Ah, Lord God! wilt thou make a full end of the remnant of Israel?" Was the prophet really transported, swung through the air, from Babylonia to Palestine? No, say the commentators with one voice, he was all the time at Tell Abib. In what way, then, did this death-dealing prophecy reach Pelatiah at the moment of its utterance, and how did the prophet straightway know of its fatal effect? These are questions which, as far as the commentaries are concerned, still remain open. I shall return to this subject in Chapter V.

The passage which immediately follows, vss. 14 ff., has given much trouble to interpreters, ancient and modern, because of the mistaken idea that the writer has Babylonian exiles in mind. It is a message given to the prophet for the faithful minority in Jerusalem, who are sneeringly counseled by their wicked and arrogant neighbors to apostatize. The prophet, after announcing the destruction of the city and the slaughter of its people, cries out, Wilt thou make an end of the remnant of Israel? He receives this answer: *Those who are like-minded with you shall be saved.* Though they must be scattered abroad, yet they shall at length be brought back, from all parts of the world. "The word of the Lord came unto me, saying, Son of man, I will save thy brethren,[11] the sharers of thy redemption, even all (those of the) house of Israel to whom the inhabitants of Jerusalem say, Get you far from Yahwè! to us the land has been given as our inheritance. Therefore say, thus saith the Lord God: When I shall have removed them far off among the nations, and scattered them among the countries, yet will I be to them a sanctuary," etc. In spite of some uncertainty in the following text (confusion of second and third person) the sense of the whole is clear. Obviously, there is no thought here of any particular country of the Dispersion. The passage is a good parallel to Is. 66:5.

In spite of the statement of transfer to Chaldea, chap. 12 contains several telltale verses which could not be permitted to stand unchanged. The people of Jerusalem were so directly addressed, in the second person, as the witnesses of the prophet's symbolic act, that slight alteration of the text was indispensable. Moreover, the customary unwillingness to *excise* any part of the sacred text caused the retention of a very significant phrase. Vs. 19 begins: "And thou shalt say *to the people of the land*"! Kraetzschmar remarks, "Der Ausdruck ist befremdlich." Hölscher, *Hesekiel*, p. 82, "Hesekiel soll seine Drohung an die Palästinenser richten." Bertholet's comment has already been quoted (above, p. 35). The personal suffixes and endings in the remainder of the verse, now third person plural, were originally second person plural, as the form of the verb in vs. 20 b shows. More important alterations were made in vss. 10–12; a passage which in its present form has been the despair of exegetes. The restored text will be given in a subsequent chapter of this volume; the translation is as follows. "Speak unto them, to all the house of Israel among whom thou dwellest say, I am your sign; as I have done, so shall be done to you; into exile,

---

[11] I had emended to אֶחָיה before discovering that Bertholet had made the same emendation.

into captivity, ye shall go. Thus saith the Lord: The one bearing this burden in Jerusalem is the prince who is in the midst of you. On the shoulder he shall bear (a burden) in the darkness," etc. It is easy to see how precisely the changes resulting in the massoretic text were necessary. Nothing has been omitted; but transposition and altered suffixes have produced chaos.

The equally troublesome chap. 24 was provided for (1) by inserting the date in vs. 1, all of vs. 2 after the address "Son of man," and the conjunction at the beginning of vs. 3; (2) by adding vss. 25–27; (3) by slight changes in vs. 24, which need not be discussed here; and (4) by a most instructive insertion—two words—in vs. 21. This last-named verse reads: "Speak unto the house of Israel, Thus saith the Lord: Behold, I will profane my sanctuary, the pride of your power, the desire of your eyes and the longing of your soul; and your sons and your daughters, **whom ye have left behind,** shall fall by the sword." Those who can imagine exiles who would *leave their children behind* (!!), in setting out for the foreign land, are free to do so. The commentators, in general, accept what is given them here; only Hölscher (pp. 130 f.) rebels. It is perfectly obvious why the redactor inserted the two words in the Hebrew text. This verse, without the addition, puts the prophet squarely in Jerusalem, speaking to its doomed people. The earlier portions of the chapter point plainly in that direction. And only two verses farther on, in vs. 23, occur two very striking phrases in juxtaposition, repeated from 4:17, where they are expressly descriptive of the mortal distress *in Jerusalem*: "Ye shall pine away in your iniquities, and be appalled[12] at one another." The description in vss. 22 f. is so obviously inapplicable to Babylonian exiles that Bertholet, Kraetzschmar, Herrmann, and Hölscher cancel the two verses, without agreeing as to the reason for their presence in our text! It is hardly necessary to explain further why the 'Babylonian' editor inserted the two words in vs. 21. His purpose was accomplished, and completely successful—until now.

At the very outset of the prophet's public ministry, and as the formal

---

[12] I believe that in the last clause the verb should be וּנְשַׁמּתָם. Observe the assonance with the verb in the preceding clause, and the similar assonance—not accidental—in 4:17 b. אֶל is for עַל, as very often in Ezekiel; cf. Job 18:20. The slightly different wording of the phrase in 4:17 is also correct.

inauguration of the work to which he had so impressively been called, he is commanded to perform certain symbolic acts of the nature described above. He accordingly predicts, in dramatic pantomime, the siege and destruction of the city and the dispersion of the people of Judea. Beyond all question, this is intended as a terrifying warning, not as a spectacle to arouse curiosity. It is delivered in the place where it would be supremely startling, and to those who would be most directly affected by the events predicted; otherwise, it is only of minor consequence, and a sad disappointment after we had been led to expect the beginning of a mighty prophecy. According to 3:15, Ezekiel had been brought to 'Tell Abib' just before these events; and in 8:3, after their completion, he is transported to Palestine and Jerusalem; we are thus expressly told where he began his great public task. But it is *only* in Judea, more specifically in Jerusalem, that such pantomimes and dramatic presentations could make the profound impression demanded for them by their position in the book. Performed in Babylonia they would be grotesque, even if we had reason to believe that 'the exiles' were greatly interested in Palestinian matters (see above, on chap. 33!). There can be no question as to the intention of the author; the symbolic acts were really performed, and were witnessed by those whose fate was therein portrayed; those whose sins are described in chaps. 5, 6, and 7, and who—certainly a few, perhaps many of them—would thereby be made to turn from their evil ways. It is easy to see that here, again, the symbolic performances and the discourses joined to them had in view neither Babylonia nor Jewish captives. The telltale phrase showing clearly the original background, almost certain to occur in each of these dramatic scenes, appears at length in 5:2.

The prophet receives the divine command to shave off the hair of his head, divide it into three parts, and make of each portion a symbol for the people. As the first of the three performances he is to kindle a fire and burn a third part of the hair *"in the midst of the city."* This means just what it says; it cannot fairly be twisted into any other meaning. The prophet's action is not merely imaginary; as in every other case of this kind, he explains its meaning to the people who have witnessed it (see vs. 12). The commentators who would have it that the fire was kindled and the bundle of hair burned "in the midst" of the tile (!) described in chap. 4 suppose a physical absurdity. Observe especially the *second person plural* in vss. 7 and 16 f., where the editor was obliged by the context to leave the words in their original form, instead of substituting the third person, as often elsewhere. The prophet is speaking directly to the men of Jerusalem, in whose presence he had performed his symbolic acts; those whom he is now warning (in the second person plural) of the approaching days of famine, pestilence, sword, and dispersion among the nations. Notice also the significant "This is Jerusalem" in 5:5. There is no need of further demonstration that in chapters 4–7, as in all those following, the prophet is in the holy city.

The location of the "valley" mentioned in 3:22 f.; 8:4; and 37:1 is now an interesting question. It certainly is not a property of the editor, but stood in the original prophecy. If it were not for the standing designation of the Kidron by the word *nachal*, it would first be thought of, because of the comparison of chap. 37 with 2 Kings 23:6. It may be that the editor substituted the word *biq'a* in these passages, because *nachal*, in such a setting as this, would at once have brought the reader to Jerusalem. Otherwise, we probably should think of the broader valley on the west side of the city.

This Chapter has shown that the Babylonian setting of the prophet's discourses is found only in a series of brief and easily recognized interpolations. A few of these are so glaringly disturbing that they have been marked off as secondary by recent commentators. The profound significance of such an insertion as that made in 24:21 cannot be too strongly emphasized, and the same is to be said of the amazingly audacious interruptions in 1:2 f. and 33:21 f. Not all of the others have received notice here; they will be brought together in a later chapter. The prophet nowhere speaks to Jewish exiles, nor does he show any knowledge of such a community. His dwelling place was Jerusalem, and his mission was to the people of the holy land, to warn and rescue those who should listen and repent.

III

THE SUCCESS OF JOSIAH'S REFORM

There is a very noticeable similarity between the sins of Judah and Jerusalem which are especially rebuked by Ezekiel and the evils which King Josiah undertook to eradicate in his great reform. This remark applies also to certain portions of the book of Jeremiah; and there is here a problem which greatly needs solution. There is sharp disagreement between the narrative of the Book of Kings and the representation of the two prophets, *as the latter are currently interpreted.* We seem to hear of a host of idolatrous and peculiar cults utterly wiped out in such a manner that they could hardly be resuscitated—and then, after the very briefest interval of time, they all are again in full force, and indeed at the very height of their prosperity. The evidence that Josiah did undertake a comprehensive reform is far too strong to be set aside. *Did his undertaking succeed?* This is a question which has perplexed commentators and historians, because of the seeming contradiction in the sources which we have. There is in fact no contradiction at all, as will be shown in the following investigation, when the utterances of Jeremiah and Ezekiel are correctly placed in order of time.

Our main source of information is the narrative in 2 Kings 22–25. The view of the narrator, beyond question, is that Josiah's reform was thorough, and that its effects were lasting; there was no repetition of the horrors which existed in the time of Manasseh (see especially 24:3). Whatever the date of the narrative, it tells us what was currently believed in Jerusalem and Judea after the fall of the kingdom. Josiah is represented as instituting the drastic measure not at all because of any new ideas of his own, or of his counsellors, in regard to the religion of Israel, but simply because of the discovery of the Book of the Law, which showed him the true character of the abominable forms of worship in which he had acquiesced. This Book, moreover, was not forthwith lost again, but remained in Jerusalem while the kingdom lasted.

Moore, *Judaism*, I, 221 f., writes: "In the seventh century foreign gods and cults flourished rankly in Israel. Manasseh earned for himself a particularly bad name by the introduction of such religions from far and wide. Under Josiah the party loyal to Jehovah had their day, and the reforms of his eighteenth year swept away the gods whom Manasseh had installed in the temple of Jehovah itself, the altars of the Queen of Heaven and the horses of the Sun, as well as the Topheth in the Valley of Hinnom just outside the city, where children were offered by fire to the divine King (Moloch)." A little farther on, in continuation of the above: "When the final catastrophe of Judah came, the prophets bade their stricken countrymen see in it the vengeance of their own god for the sins of Manasseh and his generation: Jehovah was a jealous god, who would share the worship of Israel with no other; the proof of this doctrine, enounced long ago, had overtaken them. If there were those at the moment who explained the disaster in a contrary way (Jer. 44:15 ff.), the prophetic interpretation soon came to be uncontested."

There is one cult, the history of which we are able in a measure to control, partly because the statements regarding it are so clear, and partly because it is connected with a definite locality. This is the cult of "Melek" (Moloch). It is perfectly representative of the heathen worship which Josiah set himself to exterminate, and it appears conspicuously in the discourses of Ezekiel and Jeremiah which are now in question. This Chapter will be devoted mainly to a study of the evidence derived from the utterances of the two prophets in regard to this particular 'abomination.'

The cult of Melek (Molech, Moloch) seems to have been the worst of the numerous foreign forms of worship which were imported by King Manasseh.[13] It was practised in the Valley of Hinnom at Jerusalem; and the victims were children, who were first slaughtered and then burned.

King Josiah, in the eighteenth year of his reign, undertook to root out this cult once for all, employing the same thoroughgoing method as in the case of the other 'abominations' to which he put an end. 2 Kings 23:10 narrates: "He defiled Topheth, which is in the valley of the sons of Hinnom, that no man might make his son or his daughter

---

[13] Some scholars suppose the cult to have existed before—or even long before—the time of Manasseh, referring especially to 2 Kings 16:3 (Ahaz); see however G. F. Moore, article "Molech" in the *Encyclopaedia Biblica*, cols. 3186 f.

pass through the fire to Melek." How the 'defilement' was effected is made plain in numerous other passages describing his great reform. He sacrificed the priests upon their altars, and burned their bodies; he broke the altars to pieces, and over all the places of sacrifice scattered the polluted ashes and the bones of dead men. These measures were employed by the king and his helpers in exterminating the Baal and Astarte cults and the various forms of worship of "the host of heaven," especially those introduced by Manasseh, and in destroying the "high places" throughout the land. He dealt in like manner with all the apparatus of heathen worship with which Manasseh, in his unexampled wickedness, had filled the temple and its courts.

It is plain to the reader of this account that it was looked upon as a permanent reform; and it certainly is not easy to imagine how any part of the uprooted worship, after all this destruction and especially this pollution, could be restored soon, if at all. As a matter of course it was absolutely at an end during the remainder of the reign of Josiah, thirteen years. The law had been discovered, and the king and his helpers enforced it. Josiah died in the year 608; Jehoahaz reigned three months; Jehoiakim came to the throne in 607. Yet, according to the great majority of our modern commentators and authorities dealing with the history of Israel, *all* these forms of forbidden worship, without exception, were in full operation *in the first year of Jehoiakim* and thereafter! This belief is based on certain passages in Jeremiah and Ezekiel, the before-mentioned date being obtained from the combination of chaps. 7 and 26 of Jeremiah (see below).[14] There is some mistake here. Either Josiah did not actually effect a reform, or else the commentators are in error. When did the cult of 'Molech,' in particular, come to an end? When, in other words, did the valley of Hinnom become a permanently polluted place?

As was remarked above, the belief that the abominable rites which were in vogue in the time of Manasseh and until the eighteenth year of Josiah were immediately renewed under Jehoiakim is well-nigh universal. See for example Wellhausen, *Skizzen* I, 67, 73; Smend,

---

[14] The text reads (26:1) "In the beginning of the reign of Jehoiakim," and the scene is obviously the very beginning, the first year, as the commentators in general take for granted. Subsequent years are dated; as for example "in the fourth year," 25:1 (see Duhm's Commentary); 36:1; 45:1; 46:2.

Alttest. Religionsgeschichte (1893), 270 f.; Giesebrecht, *Comm.;* Driver, *Introd.;* article "Jeremiah" by Cheyne in *Encycl. Brit.*[11], and by N. P. Schmidt in *Encycl. Bibl.;* also Rothstein, Cornill, Toy, H. P. Smith—to mention no others. As touching the Melek cult in particular, see the article "Molech" by G. F. Moore in the *Encycl. Bibl.*, col. 3187: "The worship was revived under Jehoiakim and continued till the fall of Jerusalem (Jer. 11:10–13; Ezek. 20:30 f.)." So also Baudissin, art. "Moloch" in Hauck's *Realencyclopädie;* Paton, art. "Ammonites" in Hastings' *Encycl. of Religion and Ethics;* and many others. Kennett, *Old Testament Essays* (1928), p. 47, speaks of "the rebuilding of the Topheth (Jer. 7:31)."

On the other hand Duhm, *Das Buch Jeremia*, p. 110 (on 11:10), says in regard to the theory of a general apostasy after the reform of Josiah: "Diese Ansicht von der Geschichte der letzten Königsregierungen ist schon an sich historisch unhaltbar, weil Jeremia nichts von einer solchen Art von Sündhaftigkeit Jojakims weiss." In his *Theologie der Propheten* (1875), p. 254, he had remarked that Ezekiel's depiction of the idolatrous practices has in view quite as much the time of Manasseh as that of Jehoiakim. Graf and others have held that Jeremiah, in denouncing the idolatry of his people, refers to their *past* sins, committed in the (very recent) reign of Manasseh. How, it may be asked, could these scholars dispose of Ezek. 20:31, in which the prophet declares that the sacrifices of the children to Melek are going on *at the very time of his utterance?*

The passages in Jeremiah which mention the Melek worship are 7:31; 19:5; and 32:35. They repeat one another very noticeably. The passage 19:5, which on very good grounds is denied to Jeremiah by Giesebrecht, Duhm, Schmidt, Cornill, and others, may be left out of account for the present. 32:35 is in a context which rehearses the sins of Judah *under Manasseh;* the sins by reason of which Yahwè decreed the destruction of the city and the scattering of his people. The whole passage, verses 28–35, is merely an expansion of 2 Kings 23:26 f. This also, then, may be dismissed as having no bearing on the question under discussion. We are thus left, as far as Jeremiah is concerned, with the single passage 7:31.

It is a view almost universally held in modern times that the discourses of Jer. 7 ff. belong to the reign of Jehoiakim.[15] The chief reason for this dating is the close resemblance, in general content and in some striking phrases, to the much briefer passage 26:1–6, which is expressly dated at the beginning of Jehoiakim's reign. This, however, is very slight ground for a conclusion which is opposed by stronger evidence. Even if we believe that Jeremiah wrote both passages, they certainly may belong to different occasions. The prophet, it may be supposed, had his own characteristic way of rebuking the sinful people. There were certain ideas, and forcible modes of expression, which were always present in his mind and suitable under all circumstances. Nothing could be more legitimate—supposing that these particular utterances, in the form in which we have them, were both written by Jeremiah himself and not by others[16]—than to regard the brief passage 26:1–6 as a forcible reiteration of a few of the admonitions and warnings which had previously been given under similar conditions. There are many such repetitions in the book of Jeremiah.

As a matter of fact, however, the prophecies of chaps. 7 ff. plainly belong to an earlier reign than that of Jehoiakim. The prophet, we are told in the superscription of his book (1:2), began his public ministry in the days of Josiah, in the thirteenth year of his reign; and no prophet of Judah ever had a more obvious and urgent duty than that which at once confronted Jeremiah. The king was right-minded, but the people were grievously sinning. All the abominations revived or introduced by Manasseh and continued by Amon were still in force. The Book of the Law had not yet been discovered, and the worship at the 'high places', the sacrifices of children to 'Molech' in the valley of Hinnom, the various cults of the host of heaven, even the pagan altars in the temple itself, were still as in the days of Manasseh. This is made perfectly plain by 2 Kings 22:11 ff., 16–20, as well as by what follows in chap. 23. We should suppose that Jeremiah's first utterances would be directed against these horrors; and this, in fact, is precisely what we find to be the case.

[15] Hence, apparently, the heading, "*The* Temple Address," in the American Translation of the Old Testament (1927). It is noteworthy that Streane, in the *Cambridge Bible*, after assembling the arguments pro and con, decides for the reign of Josiah.

[16] It should be remarked that Duhm, *Das Buch Jeremia*, regards chap. 26 as belonging to Baruch's biography of Jeremiah, and chap. 7 as a free expansion, by a later writer, of 26:1–6.

Chapter 11, as no one doubts, begins with an allusion to the newly discovered Book of the Law, and there follows the prophet's admonition to the people, based on this discovery. All that precedes chap. 11 belongs to the years 13–17 of Josiah's reign. So Hitzig in his day had maintained. This is clear even in regard to the passage 10:1–16, generally regarded as a later element in the book; whatever its date, it was placed here as a polemic against the unexampled idolatry of the days of Manasseh, Amon, and the first half of the reign of Josiah.

By far the clearest evidence of this dating, however, is to be found in the passage 7:29–8:3. Verse 30, as the commentators agree, refers directly to 2 Kings 21:5, 7 and 23:4 ff., the heathen cults brought *into the temple* (!) by the wicked king Manasseh. Giesebrecht, *comm.*, had previously remarked, very truly, in regard to 7:18, "Das weist auf die Regierung Manasses." On 7:30 he comments: "Zweifellos hat Jer. hier zunächst die Zeit Manasses im Auge, aber er erwähnt sie auch deshalb, weil ihr Abfall unter Jojakim erneuert worden war." There is however no evidence, nor even the slightest probability, that this utmost desecration of the temple, or anything resembling it, ever took place after the reform of Josiah. As to this, more presently. The prophet's rebuke here is addressed to his people in the time just preceding the finding of the Book of the Law. Even more important is the evidence furnished by vss. 31 ff. A striking scene in Josiah's great reform is that in which the cult of 'Molech' is destroyed, and Topheth is polluted and rendered harmless for all the time to come (2 Kings 23:10). How the pollution was effected may be seen in vss. 14, 16, and 20, where other heathen sanctuaries were defiled by covering them with the bodies or bones of dead men. In Jer. 7:31–33 the prophet is represented as speaking before the event, in the years 13–17 of the reign of Josiah, *and predicting this very thing.* Beginning with vs. 30 the passage reads as follows: "The children of Judah have done that which is evil in my sight, saith the Lord; they have set their abominations in the house which is called by my name, to defile it." (This, as we have seen, is referred by some recent commentators [Giesebrecht, Duhm] to the conditions existing in the time of Manasseh.)[17] "And they have built the high places of Topheth, which is in the valley of the son of Hinnom,

---

[17] Rothstein, in Kautzsch, *Heilige Schrift des A. T.*,[4] I, 746, regards this whole passage as later than either Jeremiah or Baruch.

to burn their sons and their daughters in the fire; which I commanded not, neither came it into my mind. Therefore, behold, the days come, saith the Lord, that it shall no more be called Topheth, nor the valley of the son of Hinnom, but The valley of Slaughter; for they shall bury in Topheth till there be no place to bury."

What was especially meant by the "slaughter" may be seen in 2 Kings 23:20: the priests of the cult of Melek are to be slain on their altars, and their bodies burned there to ashes. The prophet does not say: "Topheth shall *again* be defiled, as it was in the days of Josiah," for the obvious reason that he is speaking in the time of that very monarch (whose reform, according to 1:2, he actually witnessed!). All the surrounding context testifies to the same effect. Observe especially the introductory verse, 29, with its outburst of lamentation, and the words: "The Lord has rejected and forsaken the generation of his wrath!" Duhm, *Comm.*, does not see the connection here, but asserts: "Ein geistiger Zusammenhang existiert nicht." On the contrary, the prophet is represented as foreseeing the decree of Yahwè recorded in 2 Kings 23:26 f.; cf. 24:3 f. Because of the wickedness done in the time of Manasseh the Lord said: "I will remove Judah also out of my sight, as I have removed Israel,[18] and I will cast off this city which I have chosen, even Jerusalem, and the house of which I said, My name shall be there." And the Lord would not pardon (24:4). This is the reason of the bitter outcry of Jeremiah, purporting to have been uttered in or after the thirteenth year of Josiah, while these abominations were still in full blast and *before* the finding of the Book of the Law.

After predicting the doom of Topheth, the prophet goes on to speak of other forms of wickedness. The immediately following passage, 8:1-3, refers as plainly as does 7:18 (see the quotation from Giese-brecht, above) to the worship of the heavenly bodies which was carried on with such ardor and in such unexampled variety under Manasseh's patronage and thereafter until Josiah's eighteenth year. "At that time, saith the Lord, they shall bring out the bones of the kings of Judah, and the bones of his princes, and the bones of the priests, and the bones of the prophets, and the bones of the inhabitants of Jerusalem, out of their graves; and they shall spread them before the sun and the moon and all the host of heaven, whom they have loved,....and

---

[18] Observe that these very words are repeated in Jer. 7:15!

whom they have worshipped; they shall not be gathered, nor be buried; they shall be for dung upon the face of the earth." This describes, in the form of a prediction, precisely what is narrated in 2 Kings 23:14, 16–18, 20, as the measures taken by Josiah in exterminating the idolatrous cults. Vs. 16, "He saw the sepulchres that were there in the mount; and he sent and took the bones out of the sepulchres, and burned them upon the altar and defiled it." The graves of two of the prophets were spared (vs. 18). This was at Bethel. Not only the high places in this region and still farther to the north (vss. 19 f.), but also all the pagan sanctuaries at Jerusalem (vs. 13) were similarly defiled.

Whatever we may prefer to think as to the nature of the close relation existing between the passages in Jeremiah and the narrative of 2 Kings, there certainly can be no question of the *fact* of such relation. The prophecy fits the history like a glove, most exactly in those features which are most unusual. "History repeats itself"; but not in such a sequence of details, after so very brief an interval, and in the face of effective measures taken to prevent such recurrence. The reform was the result of the finding of the law. Did not the law continue in force? and did not the king continue to be law-abiding? Our narrative is clear and emphatic on this point. It is quite inconceivable—indeed impossible—that *all* these abominable forms of worship now recognized as call ng down the wrath of God, most of them requiring very considerable constructions, apparatus, and expert administration, and all thoroughly exterminated, should have reappeared in full swing before the mourning for Josiah was fairly over. Yet the speaker in Jer. 7 and 8 assails, *as present evils,* the cults of "the queen of heaven" and other gods (7:9, 18), the pagan altars in the temple (vs. 30), the Melek cult in the valley of Hinnom (vs. 31), and the varied worship of the heavenly bodies (8:2); and in each case the language employed implies that the abominable practice has been going on for some time. It should be sufficiently obvious that the prophet is not here speaking "at the beginning of the reign of Jehoiakim"!

Moreover, in these chapters of the prophecy of Jeremiah it is plainly indicated that *the law had not yet been found,* but the prophet is given a revelation to the effect that there is such a law. In 9:11 he cries out: "Who is the wise man, that may understand this? and who is he to

whom the mouth of the Lord hath spoken, that he may declare it?
Wherefore is the land to perish and be laid waste like a wilderness, so
that none passes through?" The prophet is given the answer to his
question in the next verse: "Yahwè said: Because they have forsaken
my law which I set before them." Accordingly, in chapter 11 the Book
of the Law, discovered in the temple, is at last before the prophet and
the people of Jerusalem.[19]

The result of this examination of Jer. 1–10 is to show that the only
ground for assigning chap. 7 to the beginning of the reign of Jehoiakim
lies in the resemblance of 7:14 to 26:6. A. S. Peake, *The New Century
Bible*, Jeremiah (1910), p. 146, says: "The identity of the two occasions is guaranteed by the presence in both chapters of the prediction
that God would make the temple a ruin like Shiloh." I would ask:
What value can be assigned to this extremely slender "guarantee" in
view of all the plain evidence to the contrary here presented? In my
own judgment, the proof is compelling, admitting of but one conclusion.
The historical setting, real or fictitious, of Jer. 1–10, including every
portion of these chapters, is the period between the thirteenth and
eighteenth years of the reign of Josiah.

In conclusion, as regards mention of 'Molech' in the book of Jeremiah, the passage 19:1–13 calls for brief consideration. Its close literary connection with chapter 7 is obvious. If it be assigned to Jeremiah
himself, it unquestionably must be dated before the 18th year of
Josiah, or else 'analyzed' into fragments. The verses (3–6) dealing
with the Melek-worship are regarded as secondary, or at all events
not belonging here, by Giesebrecht, Duhm, Cornill, Schmidt, Rothstein,
and others. As regards the relation to 7:31 f., Volz, *Studien zum Text
des Jeremia*, p. 166, holds the less plausible view that 19:3–6 is the
original, and 7:31 f. the later imitation. From purely literary considerations it is natural to suppose that 19:1–13 is a picturesquely dra-

---

[19] The passages 2:8 and 8:8 testify to the same effect, for the "law" there mentioned
with scorn and indignation *is the ritual of the pagan sanctuaries*, as the context in either
passage makes plain. The priests have their "torah" (2:8), but it deals with the service
of Baal and Astarte and other heathen deities (vss. 8, 11). The worship of Melek, in particular, was offered to Yahwè (7:31; 19:5; 32:35; Ezek. 20:25 f.), but its elaborate ritual
was not found in the Pentateuch! The priests called it a *"torath Yahwè* (8:8); but "the
false pen of the scribes has wrought falsehood" (vs. b).

matic expansion and embellishment of 7:31–34.[20] Be that as it may, there is no ground, on any literary theory, for finding in this passage evidence of Melek worship in the time of the last kings of Judah. Duhm's conclusion, quoted above, is true, on whatever critical premises it is founded: Jeremiah knows nothing of any such apostasy under Jehoiakim and his successors.

The worship in Topheth was wiped out, once for all, by Josiah. This does not mean, indeed, that he was able to permanently abolish child-sacrifice among the Hebrews. This was a very ancient and widespread Semitic custom, familiar in numerous rites, and probably existing in several forms among the Hebrews, early and late. The Second Isaiah denounces (in 57:5) some of his contemporaries who slew their children "in the valleys, in the clefts of the rocks," unquestionably as an act of worship; but the same prophet's words in 66:23 f. make it quite certain that the worship was *not* carried on in the valley of Hinnom.[21]

The conclusion gained from the study of Jeremiah is supported by all the other extant evidence. The idolatrous practices fostered by Manasseh, and accepted by priests and people in their ignorance, were not renewed in the days of Jehoiachin and Zedekiah. The ritual of the Pentateuch had been reinstated, and the sacred book remained in Jerusalem. All the kings after Josiah are characterized as "evil" in the narrative of 2 Kings, but with the use of the same stereotyped phrase; they were only such kings as to increase, rather than to mitigate, the evils which had already been decreed. The passage 2 Kings 24:2–4 deserves more attention than it has received. The narrator recounts the successive calamities which the land of Judah suffered in the days of Jehoiakim, and gives the reason for them. "The Lord sent against him bands of the Chaldeans, and bands of the Syrians, and bands of the Moabites, and bands of the children of Ammon, and sent them against Judah to destroy it, according to the word of the Lord which he spake by the hand of his servants the prophets. Surely at the

[20] I find myself unable to agree with the great majority of recent commentators in their recognition of incongruities and evidence of literary patchwork in 19:1–13. It seems to me a unit, self-consistent and effective. The manner in which it is conceived and written is, however oriental, not occidental.

[21] Baudissin, in the article "Moloch" in Hauck's *Realencyclopädie*, page 271 f., cites Is 57:5 as evidence of the continuation of the Melek cult. This, however, is a more definite claim than the evidence justifies.

commandment of the Lord came this upon Judah, to remove them out of his sight, *for the sins of Manasseh, according to all that he did;* and also for the innocent blood that he shed; for he filled Jerusalem with innocent blood; *and the Lord would not pardon."* The implication is clear, that the historian knew of no guilt of the people under Jehoiakim comparable to that which was inherited from the reign of Manasseh (cf. 23:26 f.).

An interesting side-light on this testimony is provided by 2 Chron. 33:11-19, a homiletic improvement over the narrative of 2 Kings 21. The captains of the Assyrian army carried Manasseh to Babylon, where he repented, "humbled himself greatly," and uttered a prayer which was preserved and handed down in writing. His supplication was accepted, and the Lord restored him to his kingdom. The Lord *did* pardon. Moreover (vs. 15), "He took away the strange gods, and the idol out of the house of the Lord, and all the altars that he had built." "And he built up the altar of the Lord, ... and commanded Judah to serve the Lord, the God of Israel" (vs. 16). The popular legend which thus completely whitewashed Manasseh had need to find another scapegoat, justifying the destruction of the city and the scattering of the chosen people. Accordingly, the two passages in 2 Kings which declare the *unforgiven* guilt of Manasseh's reign (23:26 f., 24:2-4) are significantly omitted in 2 Chron.; while in 36:14 ff., after the account of the wickedness of Zedekiah, the narrator adds: "Moreover all the chiefs of the priests, and the people, trespassed very greatly after all the abominations of the heathen; and they polluted the house of the Lord which he had hallowed in Jerusalem. And the Lord, the God of their fathers, sent to them by his messengers, rising up early and sending; because he had compassion on his people, and on his dwelling place; but they mocked the messengers of God, and despised his words, and scoffed at his prophets, *until the wrath of the Lord arose against his people, till there was no healing."* Thus the narrator contradicts the express statement of both 2 Kings and Jeremiah (15:4); and it is obvious that the contradiction is such as merely to confirm the conclusion derived from the other sources.

All this would have been obvious, and undoubted, if it had not been for the book of Ezekiel. The utterances of this prophet in regard to the foreign cults in general, and the cult of Melek in particular, so closely resemble those of Jeremiah, and so plainly reflect the conditions of the same period of history, that the question of date seemed to be settled. Ezekiel is dated—over and over again; and therefore, whether it seemed reasonable or not, the interpreter was obliged to conclude that the efforts of Josiah had only a very brief success, even if the report which we possess of the measures taken by him and "the party of Jehovah" is not to be pronounced a mere fiction from beginning to end. For in the book of Ezekiel, as in the first chapters of Jeremiah, the imported abominations are at their very worst.

The passages in Ezekiel mentioning the Melek worship practised in the valley of Hinnom are the following: 16:20 f., 36; 20:26, 31; 23:37, 39. Of these, the only one of especial significance for the present investigation is 20:31. "When ye offer your gifts, when ye make your sons to pass through the fire, do ye pollute yourselves with all your idols, *unto this day?* and shall I be inquired of by you, O house of Israel?" This is conclusive to the effect that the Melek worship, and the numerous other forms of pagan idolatry, are attacked as evils of the prophet's own day, not as past sins which are merely remembered. This is equally evident in the case of the heathen cults celebrated in the temple itself, those which are assailed in such a startlingly vivid manner in chap. 8 especially. The conclusion derived from the foregoing study is that these rites also, as well as the cult of Melek, existed in Israel only in the days preceding Josiah's eighteenth regnal year. So Budde, *The Religion of Israel to the Exile* (1899), pp. 183 f., well estimating the conditions in the last days of the Southern Kingdom, and remarking that the Book of the Law was still in force, writes: "The open profanation of the temple was doubtless no longer tolerated."

In conclusion, the fact must be emphasized that the people to whom this prophet is represented as speaking were conscious that it was because of their own sin that the calamity was upon them. The burning indignation with which he rebukes them in chapter after chapter is sufficient evidence of this, as also is his repeated declaration that the individual among them may find mercy; even "the wicked may turn from his way and live." "Turn ye, turn ye from your evil ways; for why will ye die, O house of Israel?" (33:11). He is addressing grievous sinners who know themselves to be such, whom he warns of a terrible catastrophe which is close at hand, in which *they themselves*—not others in a distant land—will perish utterly unless they repent.

It has been demonstrated in the preceding pages that the main items, the characteristic features, of the sin which the prophet lays to the charge of his people cannot possibly be referred to the days of Jehoia-chin and Zedekiah, nor (*a fortiori*) to the days of Jehoiakim. The re-form of Josiah was successful and its effect lasting, as would long ago have been definitely established but for the confusion which the 'Baby-lonian' editor of Ezekiel has introduced. For the date of the original prophecy we must look to a time earlier than the eighteenth year of Josiah's reign.

IV

THE DATES, ORIGINAL AND SECONDARY

The two conflicting dates at the beginning of the book, already mentioned so often, require a more particular examination here. It is by no means strange, in view of the picture of the prophet Ezekiel which has been familiar for two millenniums, that some modern scholars should have hesitated between the two dates, as to which is the original and which the later insertion. To all appearance indeed, and according to every recognized principle of literary criticism, the verses 1:2 f. are secondary; but if they are excised, the book loses a label which would be very sorely missed, for it contains not only the names of the prophet and his father and the place of his abode but also the designation of the era from which he dates his oracles. Since the name of the prophet's father is found nowhere else,[22] while each of the other items of information given here appears also elsewhere in the book, may we not suppose that the two suspected verses did originally stand at the head of the prophecy?

The question is answered in the negative by the great majority of scholars. Kraetzschmar, p. 2, states the situation admirably: 'The majority cancel vss. 2 f. (thus Hitzig, Klostermann, Winckler, Bertholet, Toy); and in fact the style of vs. 2, the interruption of the context, the change to the third person (nowhere else used, in the whole book, except in 24:24)[23] make the verses look spurious. Nevertheless it is very hard to give them up ("und doch, trotz allem, möchte man gerade sie als Buchanfang nur sehr ungern missen"), all the more because all the other prophetic writings have such superscriptions. Hence Merx, Cornill, and perhaps Kuenen, have wished to cancel 1:1. But this verse is too obviously genuine to be simply put aside' ("Allein vs. 1 trägt den Stempel der Echtheit zu deutlich an der Stirn, als dass man ihn einfach beiseite schieben dürfte"). Kraetzschmar then cuts the

---

[22] The name Būzī occurs also on a Hebrew seal of perhaps the sixth century B. C., published by me in the *Annual of the American School in Jerusalem*, Vol. III (1923), pages 103 ff. See p. 105.

[23] As will be shown in the sequel, the third person in 24:24 was introduced by the late redactor.

Gordian knot by supposing two recensions and preserving both dates, in parallel columns; a proceeding which he tries to carry out in other parts of the book—arbitrarily and unsuccessfully, as his critics are agreed.

The verdict of the most recent investigators of the book is generally in favor of verse 1 and against verses 2 f. Herrmann thinks that 1:2 and 1:3 a are separate glosses which came into the text from the margin, and that it is thus due to the second glossator that we know the full name and the priestly office of the author of the book. Rothstein, in his translation of Ezekiel in the fourth edition of Kautzsch's *Heilige Schrift des A.T.*, pronounces vss. 2 f. an insertion by "a strange hand," as has already been observed. The *American Translation of the Old Testament* (1927) encloses these two verses in brackets. Hölscher, on the other hand, would regard them as belonging to the original text, and the date in vs. 1, "in the thirtieth year," as secondary. But how is it conceivable that a definite date should be glossed by an indefinite one? It is not easy to imagine how this could happen accidentally, and the supposition of design may be dismissed as out of the question. It is on the contrary the opposite proceeding that we are to recognize here, as is now generally agreed: the very familiar supplementing of an ambiguous statement by one professing to give exact information. Verses 2 and 3 are certainly spurious, an interpolation by a later hand. It costs a pang, as Kraetzschmar says, to abandon them as unauthentic; but we have already seen that there is abundant evidence of an editorial re-shaping of this prophecy, and ill-gotten gains are better relinquished than kept.

This, however, is but 'the beginning of woes.' As all commentators have seen and said, the dates which follow, throughout the book, are all conformed to the system inaugurated by the interpolator at the beginning of the first chapter. They form a homogeneous chain and are the work of a single hand. Superficially examined, they seem to provide the greatly desired chronology, the genuine record of successive happenings; nevertheless, whether taken collectively or individually they have not pleased the commentators, have not been received with simple gratitude. Hitzig condemned the whole series as "unecht und willkürlich ersonnen." At least one date, that in 33:21, has been very generally rejected as not genuine; see above, p. 38. Others seem ill suited to the discourses at the head of which they stand; a glaring example is in 24:1. Smend, p. XXI, remarks: "Was unter die einzelnen Data gebracht wird, ist öfter von so allgemeiner Bedeutung, dass seine Verknüpfung mit einem bestimmten Tage nur als eine schriftstellerische Manipulation gelten kann." Later on, in his comment on 1:2 f., he finds himself confronted with a very serious dilemma, the same which has staggered so many others: "Nun sind aber alle dreizehn späteren Zeitangaben (8:1; 20:1, u. s. w.) nach der Vs. 2 befolgten Rechnung gemacht. Wenn Vs. 2, müssten somit auch sie sämmtlich später eingesetzt sein, was unmöglich angeht." That, however, which Smend and many others have felt to be "unmöglich" is the actual fact; the dates are certainly all worthless interpolations in so far as they belong to the chronological scheme of 1:2.

It may nevertheless be going too far to conclude that they contain no genuine element. The author of the original prophecy began his book with a date, "In the thirtieth year, the fourth month, the fifth day of the month," and it may be supposed that in the long succession of discourses, necessarily covering a considerable period, he inserted other dates from time to time. It is also to be borne in mind that the interpolator demonstrably (and in accordance with the habit of others of his class) made no more alteration of the original text than seemed absolutely necessary. The hypothesis which should be given the preference is probably this, that he found himself compelled to revise a succession of dates already provided. The *years* contained in his own formulas of dating are of course one and all false; his purpose being what it was, he could make no possible use of a chronological series beginning in "the thirtieth year," but must alter every member of it after the first chapter. The *months and days*, on the contrary, may very possibly be those of the original work.

This conjecture is given strong support by the dates themselves, in which *the months and days exhibit a regular sequence of their own, quite irrespective of the years to which they are assigned in our present text.* This very striking fact, which can hardly be accidental, seems to give us the unexpected information that the First Book (chaps. 1–39) of the original prophecy covered only the years 30–32 of its era, as over against the years 5–12 (or 27!) of the interpolator's era. In view especially of the remarkably homogeneous and closely knit character of the work—written "in einem Zuge" (Smend)—the period of $2\frac{1}{2}$ years seems much more natural than the $7\frac{1}{2}$ (or $22\frac{1}{2}$!) of the present dating. All this can best be seen in the following table, in which the massoretic readings are set over against the conjectured original dates. The former are in need of slight emendation, as is now generally agreed. The text of Ezekiel has been badly preserved, and dates are notoriously subject to accidental corruption; nevertheless the changes to be suggested are few in number and well supported.

CHAP.	THE ALTERED DATES			THE ORIGINAL DATES		
	Year	Month	Day	Year	Month	Day
1:1 f.	5	4	5	30	4	5
8:1	6	6 / 5* (LXX)	5	30	5	5
20:1	7	5	10	30	5	10
24:1	9	10	10	30	10	10
26:1	11 / 9*	(11)	1	30	11	1
29:1	10	10 / 12* (LXX)	12	30	12	12
29:17	27 / (11)	1	1	31	1	1
30:20	11	1	7	31	1	7
31:1	11	3	1	31	3	1
32:1	12 / 11* (LXX, al.)	12	1	31	12	1
32:17	12	1 (LXX)	15	32	1	15
33:21	12	10	5	32	10	5
40:1	25	1	10	35	1	10

In each case of deviation from MT in this table the reading adopted (marked with an asterisk) has other support than mere conjecture. In 8:1 the *fifth* month, instead of the sixth, is attested by the Greek version and adopted by the commentators; see Bertholet. In 26:1 the number of the month is missing, although that of the day is given. The number *eleven*, given in MT as that of the year, was certainly that of the month in the original text. The year must have been either the ninth or the tenth, as is shown by the sequence of the dates ("tenth year" in 29:1). The ninth is probably correct, since the discourses of the two preceding chapters, 24 and 25, were dated in this year, and the writer might therefore have omitted to repeat it. Very possibly it was the interpolator, hereafter to be designated as RB (i.e. the Redactor who gave the book its Babylonian setting), who transformed "eleventh month" into "eleventh year," since the latter would seem to him required by the actual history. The original author, on the contrary, is foretelling events of the more or less remote future, representing them in imagination as having already taken place.

The date in 29:1 has suffered corruption of a common type. The Greek reads *"twelfth* year and *tenth* month." This is manifestly wrong, for the twelfth year does not appear until chap. 32. MT therefore corrects to "tenth year." But the original reading must have been *"tenth* year and *twelfth* month"; since the accidental transposition is very easily made, and by this supposition the remarkable sequence in the right-hand table is preserved.

The date in 29:17 is especially interesting because of its manifest relation to that in 26:1. In the earlier chapter, dated (by RB) in the eleventh year, the utter destruction of Tyre by "Nebuchadrezzar king of Babylon" was predicted. Here in chap. 29, on the contrary, it is recorded that this king besieged Tyre without success; and the date of this latter oracle, in the regular sequence, would have been likewise *the eleventh year.* The impossibility of this collocation was clear, and RB accordingly substituted a date ("the twenty-seventh year") slightly later than that in 40:1, the last of his series. But this is not all. In the original prophecy there was no disagreement between the two oracles concerning Tyre, for in 26:7 the words "Nebuchadrezzar king of Babylon" are a manifest gloss, and the original prediction had in view quite a different conqueror. So I have argued more than once in the past (*Marti Festschrift*, p. 284; *Second Isaiah*, p. 96) and shall maintain again in a subsequent chapter of this volume. The interpolation of the name may have been made by RB himself, but it seems at least equally probable that it had been made before his time.

In 32:1, where MT has "the twelfth year," the original reading was "the eleventh year," attested by the best Greek tradition and the Syriac version and adopted by modern commentators (see Bertholet). In 32:17 the number of the month has been lost from the Hebrew, which of course originally contained it. The Greek reads "in the first month," and this is accepted by most commentators as the original reading.

At the beginning (40:1) of the prophet's Second Book, the year of the original date must have been the *thirty*-fifth. As this would not suit the chronology of RB, he substituted the *twenty*-fifth, as in our Hebrew text. The original form of this passage, as well as of all the others in which the original dating has been altered, will be given in the closing chapter of this volume.

We may now turn to the first verse of the first chapter, and the date with which the original prophecy was introduced. When the interpolations of RB are removed, the opening verses read as follows:

"It came to pass in the thirtieth year, in the fourth month, in the fifth day of the month, that the heavens were opened, and I saw visions of God. And I looked, and behold, a stormy wind came out of the north," etc.

No plausible explanation of this "thirtieth year" was possible while the spurious date (vs. 2) stood beside it and was supposed to be authentic. The numerous futile attempts to find the era according to which it is reckoned are well known and need not be reviewed here. Kraetzschmar, p. 2, before proposing his own solution of two recensions, had asked: "Bleibt wirklich nichts weiter übrig, als mit Kuenen....resigniert auf eine endgültige Lösung des Rätsels zu verzichten?" Now, however, the "riddle" is no riddle at all; the meaning of the date is obvious and certain. The year is, as usual, that of the reigning monarch, who in this case can only be one of the last kings of Judah. The following list gives their names, from Hezekiah onward, with the number of years of each reign as recorded in 2 Kings.

Hezekiah (720–693) reigned 29 years
Manasseh (692–639) reigned 55 years
Amon   (638–637) reigned 2 years
Josiah   (637–608) reigned 31 years
Jehoahaz (608)   reigned 3 months
Jehoiakim (607–597) reigned 11 years
Jehoiachin (597)   reigned 3 months
Zedekiah (596–586) reigned 11 years

The first glance at this list shows that the identity of the king in-tended in Ezek. 1:1 is perfectly assured and the dating of the prophecy quite unambiguous. "In the 30th year" could have but one possible meaning for readers of the book in its original form; or for the Jewish student of my supposition (Chap. I), who saw—as he could not fail to see—that the startling problem of Ezek. 1:1–3 had an easy solution. *The prophecy originally dated from the 30th year of Manasseh.* The content of the prophecy added certainty to certainty, as any reader of that early day must have seen as soon as the suggestion was made. The prophet's discourses are uttered in Judea, the horrible evils attacked are those belonging peculiarly to Manasseh's reign, and surely all readers believed the express statements of the Book of Kings and of the prophet Jeremiah, that it was because of the sins committed in that reign that Jerusalem and the temple were destroyed. Even modern readers will hardly need a demonstration, the truth is now so obvious; yet it will be well to present here in brief summary the astonishingly complete evidence.

The entire prophecy contained in Ezekiel 1–39 is built on the account of Manasseh's reign and its consequences which is given in 2 Kings 21:2–16. Every item provided there is utilized here in a manner which is quite unmistakable when once it is observed. The circumstances of that fateful time are perfectly reproduced; and they are circumstances which correspond to no other period in the history of Israel.

The record tells of prophecies that were uttered; the sinful people were fully informed of their guilt and given due warning of the punish-ment that was to come. 2 Kings 21:10 ff.: "And the Lord spake by his servants the prophets, saying, Because Manasseh king of Judah hath done these abominations, and hath done wickedly above all that the Amorites did, that were before him, and hath made Judah also to sin with his idols, therefore thus saith the Lord," etc. A writer who set himself to imagine what *one of these prophets* who spoke in the thirtieth year of Manasseh's reign must have said, would of necessity have produced substantially what we find here in Ezekiel.

The designation of the "idols," in the oracle just quoted (vs. 11), as *gillūlīm* may well be the reason why the word, otherwise only occasionally employed by the Hebrew writers, is used so constantly throughout this prophet's book.

2 Kings 21:8 f.: Yahwè had given his people every advantage and a glorious promise of continuance and prosperity in the land of their fathers; they had received his law and his commandments; but they would not hearken. On the contrary (vs. 15), they provoked him to anger continually, ever since the time when they were brought out from Egypt. Hence the prophet's standing epithet *beth meri*, "rebellious house," which he applies to them in 2:3 f. and thereafter constantly.

Verses 9, 11: The reproach is twice repeated, that Israel is more sinful and obdurate than the heathen nations, even those which Yahwè had destroyed (see also vs. 2). This accusation appears several times in Ezekiel, and is given prominence; see 3:5-7; 5:6 f.; 16:27 (the Philistines), 48 (Sodom).

Verses 3-7 recount the abominations introduced or fostered by Manasseh and practiced by his subjects, a list supplemented in chap. 23, in the account of Josiah's great reform.

The high places (*bamōth*). These ancient shrines of heathen worship had been removed by Hezekiah, but were restored and increased by Manasseh. In Josiah's reform they were utterly destroyed and permanently defiled, as is narrated in detail in chap. 23. In Ezekiel they are pictured as in their most flourishing condition, see especially 6:3-6, 13; 16:16, 39. If they had recently been destroyed and desecrated, the prophet would have known it and must have alluded to the fact; observe, on the contrary, how in the passages in chap. 6 *there is evident prediction of the measures taken by Josiah.*

The altars erected to Baal and to the various heavenly bodies receive in Ezekiel not only indefinite mention, as in 6:4, 6 (the "sun-images") and 18:6; 33:25 ("ye *lift up your eyes* unto your idols"), but in chap. 8 they are features of the most vivid and important description of heathen worship which the book contains. We are told in 2 Kings 21:5

that Manasseh built altars to "the host of heaven" in the two courts of the temple, and in 23:12 that these were destroyed by Josiah. In Ezekiel 8:5 ff., 16 the prophet is made an eye-witness of the incredible profanation of Yahwè's house by this flamboyant heathenism. See also 5:11. This can point only to the reign of Manasseh, to the days when the Torah was still hidden away and forgotten. It is utterly incredible—one might even say impossible—that soon after Josiah's reforms, and while the sacred book which had caused them was in the hands of the priests in Jerusalem, this amazing desecration of the great sanctuary should have been renewed. So many scholars have felt, and some have said. See above, Chapter III *passim*, and the remark of Budde quoted near the end: "The open profanation of the temple was doubtless no longer tolerated." Doubtless; and yet it is open, authorized, and shameless profanation that is pictured in the eighth chapter of Ezekiel. Hence the perplexity of those who have given serious thought to the dilemma. Hölscher, *Die Profeten* (1914), p. 306, speaking of the idolatrous performances in the temple described by the prophet, says: "Es kann sich natürlich nicht um Götzendienst der Manassezeit handeln, der durch Josia beseitigt wurde und der die Drohung Hesekiels nicht hätte rechtfertigen können, sondern nur um den Götzendienst der Gegenwart, einerlei ob der Profet darüber direkte Kunde erhalten oder ihn nur nach eigenen Erinnerungen seiner jerusalemer Zeit darstellt." It is indeed true that the prophet is attacking only present idolatry, but no hypothesis of either "Kunde" or "Erinnerungen" is tenable. The eighth chapter of Ezekiel, like every other chapter of the book, reflects only the time of Manasseh.

That misguided king "caused his son to pass through the fire," we are told by the historian of 2 Kings, and his people followed his evil example. The passages in Ezekiel dealing with the cult of Melek (Moloch) I have enumerated near the end of Chapter III, in which it was shown that this cult was utterly and permanently extirpated by Josiah; while on the other hand Ezek. 20:31 expressly declares that it was practiced *in the prophet's own day*—along with the cults of the high places, the worship of "the host of heaven," and the service of the pagan altars in the temple, all of which had been so thoroughly rooted out by Josiah. The evidence all points to one plain conclusion, and is overwhelming.

Manasseh, far from inquiring of Yahwè, practiced all kinds of divination (vs. 6). The reflection of this in Ezekiel is seen in the passages dealing with the false prophets, who follow the example of their king. The prophets of Israel "have spoken a lying divination"; see 12:24; 13:6 f., 9, 23; 22:28.

Especially striking is the charge against the wicked king, in 2 Kings 21:16, that he shed very much innocent blood, *"until he had filled Jerusalem with blood from one end to the other."* Hence, very obviously, the frequent passages in which the prophet arraigns the city as a place of wholesale bloodshed. 7:23, "the land is full of bloody crimes, and the city is full of violence." 9:9, "the land is full of blood." 24:6 and 9, "Woe to the bloody city!" See also vss. 7 f. Chapter 22 returns again and again to this accusation. "Son of man, wilt thou judge the bloody city?" (vs. 2). "The princes of Israel have been in thee to shed blood" (vs. 6). "In thee have men taken bribes to shed blood" (vs. 12). "Her princes in the midst thereof are like wolves.... to shed blood and to destroy lives, that they may get dishonest gain" (vs. 27). See, further, vss. 3, 4, 9, 13; and also 16:38; 18:10; 23:45; 33:25. In 36:18 the prophet, beholding in imagination the time *after* the destruction of the city and the dispersion of its people, represents Yahwè as saying: "I poured out my fury upon them *for the blood which they had poured out upon the land,* and because they had defiled it with their idols." It is quite needless to argue that this refers to the guilt of Manasseh and his people (because of which, specifically, according to our sources, the terrible punishment was in fact executed), and that nothing which we know or can suppose in regard to the reigns of Jehoiakim and Zedekiah could justify the remarkable emphasis put by the prophet upon this accusation of wholesale bloodshed.

The wickedness in Manasseh's time reached such a degree that a sentence was pronounced from which there could be no appeal; the Lord would not be appeased. Thus, in 2 Kings, not only in 21:12-15 but more definitely and emphatically in 23:26 f. and 24:4. Josiah, who restored the law and led the people into right ways, was a king unexampled for virtue; "yet the Lord would not turn from his fierce anger because of the provocation which Manasseh had given." And again: The word of the Lord went forth to put Judah out of his sight, because of the sin of Manasseh "and because he filled Jerusalem with innocent blood; and the Lord would not pardon." This latter passage is closely paralleled in Ezek. 9:9 f.: "The iniquity of the house of Israel and Judah is exceeding great, and the land is full of blood;.... and as for me, mine eye shall not spare, neither will I have pity." Very similar is 24:14, after the twice repeated "Woe to the bloody city!": "I the Lord have spoken it;.... I will not go back, nor will I spare, nor will I repent." In neither of the two passages can there be any question that the prophet is speaking of present evils and the guilt of those whom he addresses, by reason of which the sentence of inevitable doom is pronounced. See also 5:11;[24] 7:4, 9; 8:18; this last-named passage worthy of especial attention.

The doom pronounced in 2 Kings 21:13 f., the *complete* destruction of the city, and the scattering of its people among the nations, where they are as booty in the hand of their enemies, finds its counterpart in both particulars, as of course would be expected, in the book of Ezekiel. For parallels to vs. 13, see for example Ezek. 13:10–14 ("down to the ground, so that its foundation shall be laid bare"); 19:10–14; 22:19–22; 24:9–11; 33:27–29; and with vs. 14 compare Ezek. 7:21; 11:16 f.; 12:15; 36:4 f.; 39:23, 27.

In this connection, a word may be said in regard to the emphasis which Ezekiel puts on the power of the individual to control his own destiny, making his own choice and determining his own fate of death or deliverance, in contrast with the fate of the nation or even of the family. "The soul that sinneth, it shall die. The son shall not bear the iniquity of the father, neither shall the father bear the iniquity of the son. He that hath walked in my statutes, he that is just, shall surely live. Ye shall not have occasion any more to use this proverb in Israel, saying, The fathers have eaten sour grapes, and the children's teeth are set on edge." This is sometimes treated as the announcement of a new doctrine, as though the prophet had made an advance over the theology of his predecessors. The doctrine of the moral freedom and responsibility of the individual was not new, however. It had been repeatedly declared by the Hebrew lawgivers and prophets, all the way from the Decalogue to Jeremiah. That which was new was *the emphasis* now placed upon it, and for this there was a very obvious reason. The prophet, speaking in the time of Manasseh, foretells a

---

[24] In 5:11 b read *lō egra'*, "I will *not* diminish (the punishment)."

calamity (inevitable) which is to come, not at all upon his contemporaries, whose wickedness was the cause of it, but *upon people living a full generation later.* Here was the new situation, the new problem! Were these doomed people of the later day under condemnation in the sight of God? held guilty of the crimes of Manasseh's generation? To universal despair would be added the feeling of injustice. And what could it avail a man to seek righteousness, since the catastrophe was prescribed for all alike? No prophet ever had such need to utter individualistic doctrine, with all the emphasis given it in Ezek. 18 and 33.

There remains in the basal passage, 2 Kings 21:2-16, one verse which has not yet been considered in its relation to Ezekiel. This is verse 12, in which is repeated a phrase which occurs also in Jer. 19:3 and, much earlier, in 1 Sam. 3:11, "Behold, I will bring upon Jerusalem and Judah a calamity *such that the ears of him who hears of it will tingle.*" The manner in which the pungent declaration of this verse is played upon in the prophecy is the most striking single bit of evidence of the intimate relation of the latter to this brief record of Manasseh's reign. The prediction of woe was such as to startle and sober all who should give attention to it; but there were those who were so heedless and stubborn—"of an hard forehead and of a stiff heart," Ezek. 3:8— that the threat would slip off from them like water from a duck's back. How were those affected to whom the prophet actually addressed his message? Did the ears of these obdurate sinners tingle? Not a bit! In Ezek. 33:30-33 the prophet refers, with bitter irony, to the verse in 2 Kings. "As for thee, son of man, the children of thy people talk of thee by the walls and in the doors of the houses, and speak one to another, every one to his brother, saying, Come, I pray you, and hear what is the word that cometh forth from the Lord. . . . And lo, *thou art unto them as a very lovely song of one that hath a pleasant voice and can play well on an instrument*; for they hear thy words, but they do them not. But when this cometh to pass (behold, it cometh!), then shall they know that a prophet hath been among them."

There is still another very striking item of evidence that the scene of this whole prophecy is the reign of Manasseh. Why does 'Ezekiel' know nothing of the presence of Jeremiah in Jerusalem? The *book* of that prophet he constantly uses, though never mentioning it by name or making any formal quotation. Toy's remark, at the beginning of

V

THE CHARACTER AND DATE OF THE ORIGINAL PROPHECY

In Chapter III the conclusion was reached, through comparison with the prophecy of Jeremiah and the consistent representation of the Book of Kings, that the conditions and circumstances pictured in the uninterpolated 'Ezekiel' require a date earlier than the eighteenth year of Josiah. Chapter IV has shown, on the ground of many-sided evidence, that the original prophecy purported to date from the thirtieth year of Manasseh, that is, from the year 663 B. C. The evidence here claimed is by no means all presented for the first time in this volume; only the conclusion to which it points is entirely new. *The all-important fact of interpolation* has been recognized, and pondered over, ever since the time when the book was first published in its present form. Some of the most important of the later insertions have been all but universally recognized as such by modern scholars, namely the series of dates introduced by 1:2; and there has also been sporadic recognition and demonstration of a number of equally palpable additions (such as 19:9 a β and 24:25–27) having the same origin as the secondary dating.

It is indeed customary to subject recognized interpolations to some degree of suspicion; but in this case the information afforded by them has been felt to be too valuable to be given up (see page 58); no one, apparently, has ever made the attempt to do without them. The supposition that the interpolator may have had a purpose very different from that of the original author, even incompatible with it (as is frequently the case with interpolations), has not been entertained. The present investigation, on the contrary, has undertaken to discard the secondary elements and to ascertain the character of the work as it stood before the additions were made. The result, stated above, has appeared with the utmost clearness and certainty, and the conclusion thus established is one that cannot be overthrown.

The question now arises, however, and must be answered, whether this great prophecy was actually spoken and written in the time of Manasseh, or was composed at a later day. In the preceding chapter it was assumed without discussion (and, as will presently appear, with abundant justification) that the prophecy is built directly upon 2 Kings 21:2–16; that is, that it belongs to the class of pseudepigrapha. The unsupported argument of literary dependence is likely to go for nothing, however, when books of the Bible are under consideration. Something more is needed. The fact that a prophet of the seventh century B. C. is here represented as foretelling accurately the fortunes of Judah and its rulers down to the year 586, and in particular the precise events narrated in 2 Kings 25:1–7, might seem to be conclusive; but here also there is need of closer examination. It is obvious that a prophet who received his call and began his ministry in the year 663 might live to see or hear of the destruction of the city, and thereupon write its record and that of the main events leading up to it. It is true that all this is given in the form of dated predictions; but some recent commentators tell us that Ezekiel really wrote his book after 586, and that his recollection of the prophecies which he had uttered was 'colored' by his knowledge of the actual course of events. See Smend's note on 24:15 ff.; Bertholet, pp. XXII f., 173; Kraetzschmar, pp. 38 f., 197 bottom.

Is there any limit to the permissible vividness of such 'coloring'? When a writer tells us that in a certain year, month, and day he predicted certain very definite and important events of the future, it would seem that we must either believe what he says or else (if he habitually does this thing) characterize his proceeding as falsification of the record. The force of this alternative has of course been keenly felt, and an explanation of the most perplexing records of the seer's prescience has been found in the hypothesis of a very remarkable gift of clairvoyance possessed by him. There are, that is to say, certain instances in which the supposition of imperfect recollection is plainly inadequate. The prophet—whatever his mental endowments and habits—could never to the day of his death have forgotten whether he made the perfectly fulfilled predictions described by him in 5:2, 12; 12:5 f., 12 f.; 21:23–28 (18–23); 24:15–18 (!). There are numerous others in regard to which those who wish to do so may be permitted to believe that the prophet, in writing out the discourses of his earlier years and fitting them with dates, said to himself: "Probably I foretold this; I cannot remember; I will put it down as a prediction." But in the case of those just mentioned—three of them accompanied with symbolic pantomime performed in the sight of the people—there cannot possibly have been any failure of memory. Hence the conclusion of recent interpreters, above stated, that the prophet was clairvoyant (as *all* 'prophets' were believed to be by the Jewish writers of the last centuries B. C. and onward).

In the eyes of the modern interpreter of Hebrew prophecy, however, Ezekiel stands quite alone as a foreteller of future events. The explanation of this has by some been found in abnormal psychology, on the supposition that the prophet's physical constitution was essentially diseased. Kraetzschmar, p. V, emphasizes (with good reason) the frequency of the elements of spiritual vision and symbolic action in the prophecy. He does not however explain these, as he would explain the precisely similar elements in Daniel, Enoch, 4 Ezra, and the N. T. Apocalypse, as characteristics of a branch of Jewish literature which flourished at a much later day than the sixth century; but rather decides, in company with others, that the explanation is to be found in the prophet's morbid tendency to attacks or seizures in which he loses control of himself, being wholly possessed by his malady. While in the ecstatic condition, he hears the voices and sees the visions. (This theory is also accepted by Bertholet, see especially his note p. 19.) He is a 'pathological' subject (Kraetzschmar, p. V f.); with his constitutional weakness (krankhafte Veranlagung), he is of a nervous, passionate, excitable temperament. This last characterization, it may be remarked in passing, is curiously different from that given by the earlier commentators, including Smend and Bertholet. The latter, for example, says of Ezekiel (p. XXI), "Er ist zu sehr verstandesmässige, innerlich kalte Natur, als dass er Dichter sein könnte," and it is likely that the most of those who have read the book carefully have gained a similar impression.

The view of Ezekiel as a pathological figure, an "Ekstatiker,"was given currency especially by Klostermann's article, "Ezechiel. Ein Beitrag zu besserer Würdigung seiner Person und seiner Schrift," published in the *Theol. Studien und Kritiken*, 1877, pp. 391–439. The article is very interesting as a study in abnormal psychology; but opinions will differ as to whether it throws any light on the personal characteristics of the Hebrew author. In his summing up (p. 431) he writes as follows: "Nach diesem allen halte ich es für erwiesen, dass wir Ezechiel als einen Mann anzusehen haben, der nach einem für Katalepsie prädisponirenden Leidens- und Schwächezustande im Zusammenhange mit einer im 30. Lebensjahre gehabten aufregenden Vision von dieser eigentümlichen Krankheit ergriffen wurde. Und wenn.... zu der primären Ursache, nämlich irgend welcher Neuropathie, als secundäre hinzuzukommen pflegen aufregende Erlebnisse, religiöse Schwärmerei und mystische Speculationen, endlich auch Malariainfectionen, so dürfen wir bei Ezechiel dieses alles, wenn es zur Erklärung nöthig ist, in reichstem Masse voraussetzen." Neurosis, morbid excitement, religious mania, catalepsy, malarial infection—this is one way of rescuing the prophet.

The foregoing 'explanation'—whatever else may be said of it—leaves too much unexplained. This is especially true of the series of wonderful predictions now under consideration (predictions *unparalleled* in the Old Testament they cannot indeed be called, for those in the book of Daniel are even more detailed and striking). The discourses or narrative passages in which these predictions occur do not ordinarily suggest an abnormally excited condition of the speaker, certainly nothing that could be described as ecstasy or trance. The prophet does not speak like a man under nervous tension; on the contrary, it is the impression of art, rather than that of emotion, that these prophecies have always given and must give to the attentive reader. Any modern estimate of the literary quality of the book will bear out this general statement. The ancient and mediaeval interpreters of Ezekiel of course had no trouble with the seer's accounts of his prescience. The difficulty felt and expressed at the present day centers in the suspicious fact that nearly all the recounted examples of definite prediction deal with events and circumstances in regard to which we possess information, either in the book of Ezekiel itself or (far oftener) in other books of our Hebrew Bible, that they were exactly fulfilled. Hence the question of 'prophecy after the event' is constantly arising. The commentator struggles with this or that detailed forecast of happenings described in the last chapters of 2 Kings, loath to pronounce it a *vaticinium ex eventu*, but powerless to make it anything else.

In chap. 11 the prophet, standing in Jerusalem (whether in fact or in fancy) in the presence of certain leaders of the people, foretells the coming catastrophe and the circumstances attending it. "I will bring the sword upon you, saith the Lord; and I will bring you forth out of the midst of the city and deliver you into the hands of strangers, and will execute judgments among you. Ye shall fall by the sword; *I will judge you in the border of Israel;* and ye shall know that I am the Lord." The concluding item (11:10) unquestionably refers to the judgment at Riblah, narrated in 2 Kings 25:19–21. So all interpreters agree, and the conclusion is rendered the more certain by 6:14, where Riblah, not Diblah, is the true reading for the name of the border city. Did the prophet really foresee this in the year 592? The commentators try to avoid this conclusion by putting forth the very lame hypothesis that we are to recognize here an "Einschub"; either vss. 1–21, inserted after 586 by the prophet himself (Bertholet), or two originally separate passages, vss. 1–13 and 14–21, interpolated by a redactor (!) who thought this a suitable place to bring them under cover (Kraetzschmar, Herrmann). No better refutation of both of these suggestions is needed than the simple perusal of the closely knit, self-consistent, and utterly characteristic section of the prophecy, 8:1–11:21. As for 11:10, it is in any case prediction, not narrative. If the prophet did not recognize the difference between the two forms of utterance, or could let his memory deceive him in such an important little item as this, we must lose faith in his trustworthiness.[25]

This last remark applies equally well to the two passages 19:10–14 and 33:23–29, inasmuch as each of the two represents the speaker as foretelling definite events some years in advance of their occurrence.

[25] It has in recent years become customary to say that chap. 11, or at least the first half of it, is out of place where it now stands, since it represents Jerusalem as still standing, and filled with wicked men; whereas in chap. 9 all the sinners had been destroyed, and in chap. 10 the whole city reduced to ashes. This argument of course falls to the ground when it is understood that the prophet (who is dwelling in Jerusalem, as is shown in Chapter II) actually saw such things and persons as are described in chaps. 8 and 11, while in 9 and 10 we have mere symbolism. But even with the current view of the book the argument is unsound, for chap. 11 very obviously brings a new scene in the vision which the prophet beholds; the vision of the "man clothed in linen" has been left behind and out of account. The transition is very characteristic of Ezekiel. Similarly, in chap. 19 the mother of the princes of Israel is a lioness in vss. 2–9, and a vine in 10–14; Tyre is a city in chap. 26, a ship in 27, and a second Babylon (cf. Is. 47) in 28. In 37:1 there is a transition exactly like that in 11:1; as the vision of the sheep comes to an end, the prophet suddenly finds himself carried by the spirit into the valley of dry bones. This parallel deserves especial attention.

Chapter 19 is the lament for Zedekiah. The southern kingdom, pictured as a mother of princes,[26] appears first as a lioness, then as a fruitful vine. Under the figure of young lions the fate of Jehoahaz and Jehoiakim is set forth in the first division of the poem. The allusion to Jehoahaz is made unmistakable by vs. 4 b, and it seems to me equally certain that vss. 5–9 refer to Jehoiakim; this not merely because of vs. 5, but especially because of the plain allusion in vs. 8. Here is further evidence that the author of these prophecies was a close student of the last chapters of 2 Kings. The *"goyim* of the provinces round about" who in Ezek. 19:8 take up arms against the king and accomplish his downfall are those named in 2 Kings 24:2, namely (aside from the Chaldeans) the Syrians, Moabites, and Ammonites, sent by Yahwè "to destroy Judah." The word מְדִינוֹת, which so many have found perplexing here, is just what is required. As for vs. 9, I had long ago marked the clause "and brought him to the king of Babylon" as a palpable gloss, before seeing that Bertholet (in spite of his interpretation of all this as referring to Jehoiachin!) had done the same. The clause is metrically superfluous, the repetition of "they brought him" is very suspicious, and the word מְצֹדוֹת—whatever may be done with it—speaks loudly against any previous mention of Babylonia. The author of the poem takes no account of Jehoiachin, nor is there any reason why he should do so. That king was no "lion" in either quality or experience. He occupied the throne for three months only, and then was ignominiously pulled down from it, thus merely repeating the experience of Jehoahaz. The latter, however, was the most energetic of Josiah's sons (though not the eldest), and was the choice of the people in the crisis after his father's untimely death (2 Kings 23:30). The author of the book of Ezekiel was not especially interested in Babylonian exiles, but the later editor (RB) could not miss this opportunity of celebrating Jehoiachin and the deportation by inserting the gloss.[27]

---

[26] When the high-sounding figure of the "lioness couched among lions" is applied to Josiah's wife Hamutal it becomes a bit ridiculous. Nor would the interpretation here adopted permit this reference.

[27] I cannot see that the first word in 19:8 is "impossible," as some have termed it. We may recognize here the idiom—a military technical phrase—which is well attested in 1 Kings 20:12, inasmuch as the verbs *nathan* and *sīm* are perfectly synonymous in all such usage.

The most important part of the poem, however, is the second half. Here the fate of Zedekiah and of his kingdom is given especial prominence by the change in the symbolism. The original wording of the passage is not everywhere certain, but the main details are sufficiently clear. The last ruler of Judah kindled a fire which destroyed his shattered realm. The once-glorious kingdom withered under the divine wrath. "She was plucked up in fury,[28] she was cast down to the ground." Verse 13 then symbolizes the dispersion among the nations, which Ezekiel so often predicts.

We are told that the prophet must have composed this poem after the year 586, although 20:1 would seem to say distinctly that it was written in or before 591. Modern interpreters are very naturally concerned to avoid, as far as possible, the recognition of definite prediction amounting to clairvoyance; see especially Kraetzschmar, pp. 71 f., 156, 166. The obvious purpose of the dating, however, is to show that there *was* prediction. It may seem easy to say that this or that chapter, or portion of a chapter, was inserted later, by the prophet himself or by an editor, 'because no other suitable place for it was found'; but if the prophet thus gave himself the appearance of foreknowledge he must be charged with either criminal carelessness or dishonesty, and if it is pronounced the work of some other hand the supposition is incongruous with the clear impression made by the book as a literary composition. The same commentators who tell us at the outset that the book was written continuously, with singularly definite plan and progress, by the prophet's own hand, make significant exceptions in the attempt to avoid recognizing *vaticinia ex eventu*.

Another instance of the kind is the passage above mentioned, 33:23–29. It appears to be dated, by vs. 21, but the circumstances which it describes (as they are commonly interpreted) require a still later date. Hence Bertholet sees in vss. 23–29 and 30–33 "zwei spätere Stücke, die Hesekiel hier einschaltete, weil ihm dafür hier der beste Platz schien"; and Kraetzschmar, on vss. 23–29: "Der Redaktor hat es samt dem folgenden Stücke hierher gestellt, da er es sonst wohl nicht passend unterbringen konnte." Herrmann, p. 216, holds that Ezekiel might have learned all this from 'the fugitive'; which in view of the

---

[28] All this would not seem to apply especially well to Josiah's wife Hamutal, even if we had not read 17:8–10.

date which he, in common with the other commentators, finds in vs. 21 (emending the Hebrew text) seems truly impossible.

Among the other passages belonging to the same category are chaps. 4–7 and 17. In the former group both the destruction of Jerusalem and the subsequent conditions are described in such detail as to prove either knowledge of the actual course of events or else a quasi-superhuman power of looking into the distant future. These chapters expressly and unmistakably constitute the beginning of the prophet's ministry, containing his first utterances and describing his first symbolic performances in the sight of the people. The language employed is such as to give the reader the distinct impression that the seer was then and there given the complete substance of the message which he uttered, and told the meaning of the symbolic actions which he performed. As to this there can be no question; see 4:15 ff., 6:11 ff. If in fact he only understood his prophecy "after 586," why did he make the record in such a way as to give a false impression?

Oracles against Edom, charging the Edomites with active hostility after the destruction of Jerusalem, making capital for themselves, with jeering exultation, from the calamity of Israel, are frequent in the Old Testament, and are of relatively late date. The passages in Malachi, Obadiah, Jer. 49, Amos (1:11 a late insertion), 1 Esdras 4, and Psalm 137 are very familiar. The rivalry with the Edomites was ancient, and their advance into Southern Judah in the sixth century and thereafter so increased the feeling against them that by the time of the Second Isaiah (chaps. 34 and 63) "Edom" had become a symbol of all the enemies of Yahwè. The encroachment upon Southern Palestine was relatively slight, however, as is shown by the fact that Jerusalem and the principal cities of Judah continued to be Hebrew and never contained any strong Edomite element. 'In the ninth year of the captivity,' 24:1, or even 'in the twelfth year,' 32:1 and 33:21, it could not have been known to 'Ezekiel,' unless by divine revelation, what policy the Edomites (and also the Ammonites and Moabites, 25:3 and 8) were going to pursue. Twenty years after the fall of Jerusalem it probably would have been evident what they *had done*; but their action, whatever it was, cannot have been of a nature to be taken speedily and all at once. Edom was not a man, who could announce his policy, but a country and a people; and their movement northward, as the result unquestionably shows, was not an armed invasion, but a gradual pushing forward, extending over many years. The prophecies in Ezekiel 25 and 35 are not only 'after the event,' but a long time after. Far more striking than any of the examples thus far given is 12:12 f. The prophet, by means of a very elaborate pantomime executed in the sight of the people (the people of Jerusalem originally intended, see Chapter II) foretells the events narrated in 2 Kings 25:4–7: the breaching of the wall of the besieged city; the flight of Zedekiah by night, accompanied by the remnant of the Hebrew army; the capture of the king by the Chaldeans and the scattering of the force accompanying him (cf. 2 Kings vs. 5 with Ezek. vs. 14); and the blinding of the king's eyes before his transportation to Babylon (2 Kings vs. 7 and Ezek. vs. 13). Ezekiel's pantomime is described in vss. 3–7. It is finished at night, "in the dark"; and on the following morning (vs. 8) the curious people ask him what it is all about. He gives them the full interpretation, in unmistakable terms.

Here is a staggering example of 'second sight'—and the most of the commentators are duly staggered. Herrmann (p. 77) queries whether vss. 12–14 may not be a later 'redactional' insertion. Bertholet (p. 65) puts the unavoidable question, whether this is not a prophecy after the event, but is unwilling to answer the question squarely in the affirmative; it would be, he feels, "die dürftigste Erklärung, die man den ausdrücklichen Worten Hesekiels kann angedeihen lassen." Kraetzschmar (p. 126) maintains that Ezekiel could not thus have foretold the fate of Zedekiah, 'because the prophets were not wont to make such definite and special predictions' (but was not Daniel a prophet?). Both he and Bertholet have the hardihood to decide—as in the other instances—that the prophet, at the time when he performed his symbolic act, did not know what it signified; but learning the meaning of it after the destruction of Jerusalem, he decided, in writing out the record of his prophecies, to say that he had known it all the time. The people asked him, "on the following morning," and he told them. Such a proceeding on the part of Ezekiel would be more justly characterized by the phrase "eine freche Lüge" (quoted from Smend, more than once, by these commentators) than by Bertholet's milder "eine gewisse Unwahrheit oder zum mindesten ein starkes Zurücktreten des Unterscheidungsvermögen zwischen äusserm und innerm Geschehen."

No prophet or private citizen who had gone through such a strange performance as that described in vss. 3–7 could possibly fail to remember whether he understood what he was doing. And Ezekiel says, I foretold definitely the fate of Zedekiah.

There is, moreover, another series of passages in which the supposition of clairvoyance—if this is really a seer prophesying at Tell Abib—is acknowledged to be unavoidable. In 24:1 he is shown a vision of the momentous event then taking place in far-off Palestine. The Chaldean armies are beginning the siege of Jerusalem. He writes down the date. Smend's comment has met with general acceptance: "Dass Ezechiel das damals wirklich gethan habe, bezweifeln oder gar dreist läugnen, heisst ihm eine freche Lüge zuschieben, und dazu hat keine Kritik ein Recht, zumal Aehnliches auch sonst geschichtlich bezeugt ist. Swedenborg wusste ebenso von einem Stockholmer Brande im Jahre 1759." Very true. Such an occurrence is marvellous, but isolated cases of the sort have seemed to be well attested. We could not in fairness deny to Ezekiel what we credit to Swedenborg.

In 33:21 f. is narrated the incident of "the one that had escaped out of Jerusalem" and the tidings which he brought to Tell Abib. Vs. 22: "Now the hand of the Lord had been upon me in the evening, before he that was escaped came, and he had opened my mouth." This means (cf. 24:26 f.!) that the prophet had a divinely given premonition of the approach of the man; a revelation received by him while in a state of "Ekstase" (so the commentators; see also Kittel, *Geschichte des Volkes Israel*, III, 1927, pp. 258–263).

A still more surprising incident—on the supposition of a prophet in Babylonia—is narrated in 11:13. Ezekiel utters at Tell Abib a terrifying prediction; Pelatiah ben Benaiah hears it, at the moment of its utterance, in Jerusalem and falls dead; the prophet, aware of this, immediately cries out. Was Pelatiah, also, an 'Ekstatiker'? The comms. have another explanation. The man's sudden death was not caused by the prophecy, but merely happened to occur at just the time when it was uttered. Ezekiel knew of the occurrence by virtue of his gift of 'second sight' (so Be., Kr., Herrm.). This instance is especially amazing because it is not clear how the mere knowledge of Pelatiah's death on a certain day could have an important bearing on the prophet's mission.

The passage 24:15-18 tells of the sudden death of the prophet's wife, and of the divine message by which he was forewarned of the coming affliction. Here, again, is recorded the startling phenomenon of knowledge before the event. *Was* he really told in the morning that his wife was to suffer a fatal 'stroke' (*maggēpha*) on that same day? So Smend queries, and concludes: "Kuenen hat vielleicht Recht, wenn er meint, dass die vorherige Ankündigung des Todesfalls durch Jahve nur zur schriftstellerischen Form der Darstellung gehöre." There certainly is no ambiguity in the "literary form," as any one can see who reads the Hebrew text. And (if Ezekiel in Babylonia is the author) there are only two possible alternatives: to believe what is clearly said, or to charge the writer with conscious dishonesty.

The list of these wonderful occurrences is so long, it is no wonder that the interpreters of Ezekiel do their best to cut it down, while expressing their uneasiness. Smend could defend the narrative of *one* such case by referring to the incident in Swedenborg's life. Rothstein (in Kautzsch's A. T.), in the Introduction to chap. 12, says in regard to the prediction of Zedekiah's fate, 'This is not the only occasion on which the prophet gives evidence of an extraordinary power of foreseeing future events; we therefore ought not to refuse belief on dogmatic grounds.' It was this prediction, the most detailed and the most emphatically attested of all, that Kraetzschmar (who refused to give it credence) characterized as unparalleled in genuine Hebrew prophecy (see above). We know that Ezekiel's forecast of the future, introduced by "Thus saith the Lord," was not infallible. He prophesied in 29:10-12 that Egypt would for forty years be utterly uninhabited (apparently an exaggeration of Jer. 46:19); in 26:14, 21, that Tyre would not only be completely destroyed by her besieger, but would never be rebuilt (apparently an exaggeration of Is. 23:15 ff.);[29] and some other details in his prophecies in regard to foreign nations are likewise inconsonant with the reality. The predictions belonging to this latter class, to be sure, are hardly intended to be taken literally; they have the flavor and high color of the apocalypse. It is by the long series of incidents out of the prophet's own personal experience that the interpreters of Ezekiel are forced to the wall.

[29] It is now commonly held that the prophet in 29:17-20 corrected his prophecy of chap. 26. This is not the case, however, for the words "Nebuchadrezzar King of Babylon" in 26:7 are a mistaken insertion in the text by a later hand; see below.

It may not be out of place to repeat here, by way of illustration, an alleged dialogue in a court of law, where the prosecuting attorney was trying (in vain) to induce the witness for the defence to use the word "incredible," or its equivalent.

Attorney. If you were told, by some one not known to you personally but believed to be trustworthy, that a man had fallen from a fourth-story window onto a stone pavement without suffering the slightest injury, what would you say?

Witness. I should call it a marvel.

Attorney. Marvel, indeed! perhaps not utterly impossible. Suppose you were then told that the same man fell from the same window a few days later, and this time also without any ill effects.

Witness. I should call it a coincidence.

Attorney. Now consider your reply. If the same narrator were to tell you that this "marvel" had occurred a *third* time, what would you say?

Witness. I should call it a habit.

Our commentators find themselves obliged to postulate for Ezekiel an utterly incredible "habit,"[30] because (accepting the given historical setting and dating) this is the only way to save his reputation for honesty. Even so, not one of the commentators quoted in the preceding pages is willing to accept as genuine more than a small portion of the cases in which the book, as it stands, plainly professes to give evidence of the seer's foreknowledge through divine revelation. A few are admitted, because there obviously is no escape from them; the rest are variously avoided; not quite convincingly, as we have seen.

Accepting the presuppositions required by the book in its present form, an Ezekiel at Tell Abib and a genuine prophecy of the sixth century B. C., it is not likely that any one could deal more successfully than our modern interpreters with the array of foreseen events and precisely fulfilled prophecies. But it is not necessary to put credulity to so severe a test. It will appear more and more clearly that the habit which is to be recognized is not the clairvoyance of an exiled epileptic, but a literary procedure made familiar by other Jewish authors.

[30] I speak here for those (including each and all of the commentators whom I have quoted in the preceding pages) who regard the last chapters of Daniel as representing a well known and important class of Jewish literature, and not as containing the actual predictions of a man who, living in Babylonia in the sixth century B. C., foresaw in complete detail the course of Seleucid and Ptolemaic history.

The framework of these discourses is not true history, not genuine autobiography; both framework and fabric are the product of imagination kindled by religious fervor. This is the mode of teaching of which we have such inspiring examples in Daniel, 4 Ezra, and the Book of Revelation. The author of our prophecy did not live in the time of Manasseh. Writing at a later day, he endeavored to enforce the lesson of that uniquely wicked and fateful reign by conceiving what one (presumably the first) of the prophets mentioned in 2 Kings 21:10 ff. and 24:2 had said. And just this, indeed, a faithful teacher of the people under Manasseh might well have uttered, if the Hebrew 'prophet' had been in reality, as he was imagined in a subsequent age, a man whose primary office, under divine inspiration, was to foretell the future.

In one passage only does the writer fall completely out of the rôle which he has assigned himself, namely in 38:17, where *he looks back upon the closed company of the Prophets of Old:* "Thus saith the Lord God (to Gog): Art thou he of whom I spake in old time by my servants the prophets of Israel, who prophesied in those days for many years that I would bring thee against them?" It is clearly impossible to suppose that a prophet who lived while the Southern Kingdom was still standing, but little later than Isaiah and earlier than Jeremiah, could speak thus of his associates; nor could an 'Ezekiel of Tell Abib,' constantly quoting Jeremiah (who would have been his contemporary), whom he certainly regarded as a prophet. Herrmann, in his comment on 38:17-23, writes: "Der dieses Stück einleitende Satz befremdet sehr im Munde Ezechiels. Er klingt doch zunächst so, als ob die Profeten und ihre Voraussagungen, deren Erfüllung der Verfasser dieses Satzes in dem von Gog gesagten sieht, in weiter Ferne zurücklägen." Certainly; and many others have said the same. In fact, the author of this prophecy *did* look upon the company of the Hebrew prophets as belonging to the remote past. That which made it easy for him to fall out of his rôle in this one place was not the consciousness of his own remoteness in time from these famous teachers of Israel, but rather, the late date of the tremendous invasion of 'Gog' (Alexander the Great, see below), who, according to the popular belief, had made his appearance *after the last of the prophets had passed away.*

There is plenty of evidence to show that the original book of prophecy purporting to come from the time of Manasseh was composed many generations after the destruction of Jerusalem. The most of the items in the list have long been discussed—and found troublesome— by the interpreters of Ezekiel.

The mention of Persia (*Paras*) in 27:10 and 38:5 is a famous puzzle. How could Ezekiel make this casual mention of the Persians before that people had made its appearance on the stage of history? Elsewhere in the Hebrew scriptures the name occurs only in Daniel, Esther, and the writings of the Chronicler. The answer is, that the book of Ezekiel was composed in the same very late period as the books just named.

Another troublesome passage which suggests itself in this connection is 8:17, where one of the pagan cults in the temple at Jerusalem is described. "About five and twenty men" stand in the inner court, with their faces toward the east, and they worship the sun (vs. 16). Vs. 17 then ends by saying, "*they put the branch to their nose.*" This is a remarkably plain allusion to a well known feature of the Persian ritual *in the worship of the sun*, the devotee holding a branch, or bundle of twigs, before his face. See the literature referred to in the commentaries on the passage, and in Gesenius-Buhl, s.v. *zemōrah*. It is plainly impossible that an Ezekiel of the sixth century should have seen or imagined a Persian cult in Jerusalem. The straits to which commentators can be driven in the attempt to avoid an obvious fact which *must not* be accepted can nowhere be better illustrated than in the treatment of this passage. It would be interesting to give examples, if space permitted.

The *language* of the book marks it distinctly as belonging to the very latest stratum of Old Testament literature. Smend, pp. XXVIII f., set forth at some length the evidence of lateness in the style and diction of the book. One or two of the subsequent commentators have repeated the general estimate, that the Hebrew is not that of the classical period, but without carrying the evidence farther or drawing from it any conclusion. There doubtless has been the feeling that no conclusion *could* be drawn, and that therefore investigation is useless, inasmuch as the date of the seer of Tell Abib is early, and there is no apparent reason why he should not have written the language of his own time. Cornill's *Introduction*, for instance, has nothing to say in regard to the variety of Hebrew written by the author of this prophecy. Yet it is a very important matter. The Hebrew of the late seventh century, and early sixth, was as pure and 'classical' as at any other time, judging from the specimens which we have. A highly educated man, well versed in the literature of his people, who flourished in the time of Josiah and Jehoiakim, would certainly be expected to write the language which we see and admire in Isaiah, the oldest parts of Jeremiah, the narratives in 2 Kings, and Deuteronomy. A sojourn among Israelite captives in a foreign land might well make him more careful for the purity of the sacred tongue; though it more probably would have no effect on his literary usage (so Cornill, in Selle, p. 40).

What *is* 'late' Hebrew? Our materials for answering the question are meager and imperfectly understood, and a sharp definition is hardly possible. Driver, in the last edition (1913) of his *Introduction*, has some remarks touching this subject. In making his characterization of the language of the 'Priestly' stratum of the Pentateuch he says (p. 156): "The real change in Hebrew style does not begin till a later age altogether." And a little farther below: "The change is beginning (c. 450) in the Memoirs of Nehemiah and in Malachi; but Aramaisms and other marks of lateness (esp. in syntax) are abundant only in works written after this date—Esther, Chr., Eccl., &c." But Malachi and the (genuine) Memoirs of Nehemiah are classically elegant in comparison—or rather, in contrast—with Ezekiel. There was no *significant* change in literary Hebrew as early as "c. 450." Centuries earlier than this, its vocabulary had begun to be enlarged from without, chiefly from the neighboring Aramaic, a great language with its own literature. This was a slowly increasing process, so that, for example, the elegant diction of the Second Isaiah (c. 400) includes a noteworthy number of Aramaisms. This, in itself, implies no lack of native vigor. We do not pronounce such languages as the English and the classical Arabic feeble or corrupt because of their remarkable ability to borrow and assimilate foreign words. Real deterioration in the language of the Old Testament did not set in until well on in the Greek period, when Hebrew rapidly lost its hold as the speech of the people and was replaced by Aramaic. Even after this time, indeed, excellent Hebrew was occasionally written by Jewish scholars.

Driver, *ibid.*, p. 156, expresses his opinion (with which all will agree) that the language of Ezekiel shows more signs of lateness than P. He is however far from doing justice to the extent of the difference—because of his belief, the universal belief, that the prophecy was written in the early part of the sixth century. His own explanation of the solecisms in the book will not satisfy all students of the subject. He writes (p. 157, note): "The incorrectnesses which appear from time to time in Ezekiel are due probably, partly to the fact that, as a prophet mingling with the people, he was exposed to influences from which the priests were generally free." It will, I think, eventually be recognized by all students of the Hebrew Old Testament that the chief reason why the language of Ezekiel appears so decidedly inferior to that of the Priestly sections of the Pentateuch is that it is later—much later.

There is a very useful little treatise on the Aramaic element in Ezekiel by Friedrich Selle, entitled *De Aramaismis libri Ezechielis*, published (as a dissertation) at Halle in 1890. It has been used to some extent by commentators, but the importance of the subject has not been appreciated. Recent textbooks of Introduction to the Old Testament literature (Driver, Cornill, Meinhold) in their lists of books useful for the study of this prophet do not mention Selle's monograph. This is hardly surprising, for, while the date of composition of Ezekiel is unquestioned and regarded as unquestionable, the utterly inexplicable phenomenon of a strong Aramaic element in the book might well be handed over as a puzzle to the philologists—who, for their part, could feel little interest in it. Selle himself (it is perhaps hardly necessary to say) is able to draw no general conclusion from the facts which he presents.

It is of course impossible here to do more than touch upon the subject. The Aramaisms of the book are multiform and pervasive, and cannot be described in small space. It is not here chiefly a matter of borrowed words, but rather of structural features; those innovations in morphology and syntax which signify degeneration; such a collection of phenomena as will be searched for in vain in any Hebrew writing prior to the very latest books of the Old Testament. As for the borrowed words, Selle, after presenting and briefly discussing his own list, on pages 40–47, remarks that many other locutions are either suspected of being Aramaisms or, as not yet adequately investigated, are capable of suspicion, and concludes: "Si omnia velim enumerare, dies me de-ficiat, nisi fere totum lexicon Ezechielicum scribi necesse fuerit." This of course is exaggeration, and some of his attributions are at least doubtful; but even so, the list is most impressive and instructive.

The following grammatical features, illustrating the transition from Hebrew speech to Aramaic, are worthy of especial notice (I give the page numbers in Selle's pamphlet). The very characteristic substitu-tion of dentals for sibilants, in the root-consonants; 14 f. This change, the history of which we can trace in the very considerable body of Aramaic papyri and inscriptions known to us, *is unexampled until the latter part of the fifth century,* and does not begin to appear frequently until after the fourth century. There is a clear example in 35:13, supported by context and parallelism as well as by very common Aramaic usage. Another, not noticed by Selle, is the word קְטֻרוֹת in 46:22, in its meaning and the manner of its use exactly corresponding to קְצֻרוֹת, in 42:5. In the one passage, the word is still given in its Hebrew form; in the other, the Aramaic dental has taken the place of the sibilant. In both, the meaning is *"smaller,"* literally, "reduced in size." (It may be remarked here, incidentally, that the supposition of *one* Hebrew root קצר, with the original meaning "contract, bind, cut short," etc., accounts perfectly for every known use of words contain-ing these radical letters.) I believe that קפדה, "distress," 7:25 (Selle, p. 46), is still another example, the Semitic root denoting "contraction, compression." See my note on the forms of this root, in *The Second Isaiah,* pp. 286 f., 292 f.—The insertion of *nun* or *resh,* as a mere phonetic expansion, or resolution of the doubling of a consonant, in nominal or verbal forms; 17, 26. This is especially common in Biblical Aramaic.—The employment of Aramaic pronominal forms; 17–20.—A noticeable adoption of certain noun formations characteristic of the Aramaic language; 31 f.; also, the occasional use of its inflectional end-ings; 32–34. This includes both the fem. sing. written with *aleph* and the masc. plur. *-īn,* each occurring more than once. (With the *kullā* in 36:5 compare Dan. 4:25.)—Among verbal forms, there is an *af'el* in 36:5; a *hof'al* participle (canceled by the Massorites) in 46:22;[31] and a

---

[31] The obvious reason of the cancellation is the impossibility of making any use of the word *where it now stands.* In both form and meaning it is perfectly suited to this context, and the only plausible supposition is that it was written by the author of the book. I

most significant series of hybrid infinitives: of the Aramaic *peʻal* in 36:5, *migrash* (!); regular *paʻel* forms in 22:4; 26:21; 27:36; 28:19; 34:12; 35:12; a surprising *hafʻel* construct in 24:26, *lĕhashmāʼūth* (!); and in 17:9 a mongrel form, half Aramaic and half Hebrew. There is also an example of the participle of a middle-weak verb employing *aleph* as a middle consonant, 16:57. For all these see Selle, 23, 24, 28, 32. The characteristic Aramaic loss of final *aleph* in verb roots is illustrated, with many examples, p. 29.

To mention a few other features: The constant confusion between the prepositions *ʼel* and *ʻal* comes from the time when the former, not used in Aramaic, was disappearing from the popular speech.—In 16:43 the Aramaic interjection is undoubtedly to be seen; 34.—*Lamed* introducing the direct object; 35.—The employment of a proleptic pronoun, in the characteristic Aramaic manner, in 14:4; 36. This suffix pronoun (fem. third person sing.), like not a few of the forms listed above, has been 'emended' away by the majority of recent commentators, especially since Cornill's arbitrary rewriting of the text of Ezekiel. The testimony of LXX, Syr., or Targum is likely to be worthless in such cases as this, for they conceived it their duty to interpret, rather than to preserve curiosities, and were satisfied to smooth over difficulties. Moreover, they are not independent witnesses.—The interrogative clause. In Aramaic, interrogative sentences commonly have no introductory particle, in this respect differing from the Hebrew. (In the latter, to be sure, in O. T. usage, the particle is occasionally omitted; and some passages, intended as questions, have accordingly been misunderstood.) In Ezekiel, the usage which appears is just what might have been expected from knowledge of the writer's Aramaizing tendency; he almost always employs the Hebrew particle, but now and then omits it, in the Aramaic manner, *where the context plainly shows that a question must have been intended.* Thus 11:13, Wilt thou utterly make an end? 15:5, Shall it yet be fit for service? 17:9, Shall it prosper? (It is not necessary to suppose corruption of the text here, however easy the supposition.) 18:13, Shall he then live? The same question again in

---

believe that it originally stood immediately after *qetūrōth* (the word mentioned above), and that it signified "rectangular," lit. "provided with corners" (cf. the *puʻal* participle in Ex. 26:23 and 36:28). Having been accidentally omitted in copying, it was inserted by the scribe at the end of the verse—a thing which has happened elsewhere.

vs. 24: Shall he do such abominable things as the wicked man does, and live? 33:26, and shall ye inherit the land?

There is a certain and most important example of this usage in 20: 23–26, a passage which seems to have been universally misunderstood, at least in modern times. The prophet is rehearsing the long history of Israel's grievous iniquity, and of Yahwè's wonderful forbearance and unceasing provision for the welfare of his people. He refers again and again to Yahwè's solemn promise (I lifted up my hand, i.e. I swore; a phrase taken from Ex. 6:8 and Num. 14:30) to bring the children of Israel back to the land of their fathers. He mentions the successive times when the God of Israel was sorely tempted to renounce this promise, and instead to 'lift up his hand' to abandon his people, *but did not do so*. They had merited nothing better than to be destroyed in Egypt (vs. 8); but they were rescued. They were given 'statutes and judgments by which man may live'—*laws which never were repealed*. When in the wilderness, they richly deserved to be left to perish (vs. 13); but Yahwè, for his name's sake, held to the oath which he had long ago taken. Vs. 15: *"I did indeed* swear to them," namely, to the men of one sinful generation, "that I would not bring them into the land." The accusation is then gradually brought to a climax. The children sinned like their fathers. Even after Yahwè brought them into the land which he had 'lifted up his hand' to give them (vs. 28), they hastened into every sort of idolatry, worshipping the deities of the heathen at the high places, and even offering their sons to Molech (vs. 31). Had not Yahwè done everything possible, to preserve them as his own people, and to keep them from straying? The answer to this question is given in vss. 22 ff. The purpose of vss. 23–26 is to say, with the utmost possible emphasis just before the final indictment, that the unparalleled sin of the people was committed in spite of Yahwè's forbearance and the special provision which he had made for their welfare. This purpose is, or should be, placed beyond doubt by the connection with vs. 22 on the one hand and with vss. 27 f. on the other. Yahwè declares (vs. 21) that he was ready to pour out his fury upon them in the wilderness. "Nevertheless I withdrew my hand, and wrought for my name's sake, that it should not be profaned in the sight of the nations, in whose sight I brought them forth. *Did I at all*[32]

---

[32] Repeating the emphatic phrase used in vs. 15, but now, with even greater emphasis, in the form of a question.

swear to them in the wilderness, that I would scatter them among the nations, and disperse them through the countries?" By no means; he did nothing of the sort, nor does the record tell of any such oath. Instead of scattering them among the foreign peoples round about, he kept them separate, and brought them safely to the promised land. A similar question in vs. 25: "*Did I at all* give them statutes that were *not* good, and judgments whereby they should *not* live?" This is stern irony; see the preceding verse, and compare vss. 11 and 13, where the speaker had characterized the laws given to Israel. Vs. 26 proceeds, specifying the most notorious of the evils of Manasseh's time: "Did *I* defile them through their offerings, in that they caused all their firstborn to pass through the fire?" The answer expected is of course negative, as in the other cases. The customary reading of declarative sentences,[33] instead of interrogations, brings the interpreter into very grave difficulties, without the compensation of any religious or moral gain.

So much for the Aramaic element in Ezekiel. I have not here presented any list of the very numerous loanwords, and I have omitted much of the remaining material that Selle deemed worthy of inclusion. The evidence given in the preceding pages, however, tells a plain story. The language of the book is not only late, it is very late. The 'significant change' in the literary Hebrew certainly appears here to have progressed distinctly beyond what we observe in the writings of the Chronicler. The stage of development is more nearly that which is illustrated in Daniel, Esther, and Ecclesiastes.

We may turn now to the literary relations. The evidence here is far stronger and more unequivocal than scholars have been wont to suppose. Of itself, indeed, and without the help of any of the evidence heretofore presented, it is sufficient to stamp Ezekiel as one of the very latest of the Old Testament writings.

The author of the work, as its interpreters have long observed, is a man of many books, one who has at his disposal a library of sacred scripture, and habitually shows acquaintance with it. We recognize in him "den gelehrten Schriftsteller" (Meinhold, *Einführung in das A. T.*, 259). Driver, 296: "Ezekiel's book evinces reflection and study." Bertholet, XVII: "Ein Element, das Hes. vor seinen Vorgängern aus-

---

[33] Thus even in Ps. 106:27!

zeichnet und das gerade dem Apokalyptiker zu eignen pflegt, ist die Gelehrsamkeit." He has studied, and makes literary use of, those by whom God "spoke in old time, the prophets of Israel, who prophesied in those days"; and the prophet *to whose prediction he is alluding in this very passage*, 38:17, namely Jeremiah (the prophecy 4:3–6:30; it is only necessary to compare 4:6, 13, 24; 5:15, 17 with Ezek. 38:4, 6, 15, 16, 20; 39:2) is one whose book he very frequently uses, as already observed. He is deeply versed in the laws of Israel, especially those portions which belong to the latest strata of the Pentateuch.

His very close relation to the "Holiness" legislation, in particular, has long been the subject of discussion, of which the conclusion can only be, that he, not the Code, is the borrower. This was convincingly demonstrated by L. B. Paton in the *Presbyterian Review*, Jan., 1896, pp. 98 ff., and it is not easy to see how an unprejudiced argument can reach any other result. The same is true of Ezekiel's relation to the (supposed) "Priest's Code," though scholars of the modern school have very naturally found it difficult to admit this. Driver, p. 145, remarks: "However doubtful it may be whether Ezekiel presupposes the *completed* Priest's Code, it is difficult not to conclude that he presupposes *parts* of it. In particular, his book appears to contain clear evidence that he was acquainted with the 'Law of Holiness.'" And after giving some illustration he proceeds: "In each instance he expresses himself in terms agreeing with the Law of Holiness in such a manner as only to be reasonably explained by the supposition that it formed a body of precepts with which he was familiar, and which he regarded as an authoritative basis of moral and religious life." The plain fact, as one day will be generally recognized, is that the author of the book had before him the completed Pentateuch, in the very form in which it lies before us at the present day. There are some sound observations touching this matter in J. Oscar Boyd's little pamphlet, "Ezekiel and the Modern Dating of the Pentateuch," reprinted (1908) from the *Princeton Theological Review*.

The wider literary question has been brought into a new phase, while important aid to the criticism of this prophecy has been provided, by the recent work of Professor Millar Burrows, of Brown University, entitled *The Literary Relations of Ezekiel*, published (as a Yale dissertation) in 1925. Burrows has made a diligent collection of the

Old Testament passages in which literary influence from or upon Ezekiel might well be supposed, and has given them a careful discussion. I need here hardly do more than refer to his treatment of the subject and express my own agreement with his final result. He concludes, that from indications of literary influence alone Ezekiel would appear to be one of the very latest books of the Old Testament.

Burrows' argument has received little attention as yet, and the few who have noticed it have hardly done it justice. Curt Kuhl, reviewing the book in the *Theol. Literaturzeitung*, Mar. 17, 1928, justly praises its scholarly caution and reserve, but will not admit its right to reach a conclusion. How is it possible, out of so many repetitions of "perhaps," to extract a probability? *Careful* examination of the book, however, will show that in several instances the verdict of Ezekiel's dependence on late O. T. writers goes beyond a "perhaps." In other cases, where literary dependence of some sort is recognized by modern commentators, the conclusion is stated: 'If this is true, as it seems to be, Ezekiel is the borrower.' Some will feel, too, after examining the evidence here and there, that while Burrows never overstates, he sometimes understates. He well characterizes the style and habit of this author, both in his concluding estimate and also in his introductory pages, where he describes Ezekiel's very characteristic manner, constantly illustrated, of expanding and embroidering upon passages in the works of his predecessors. The conclusion stated on p. 103 will surprise many, but I think that it will stand the test of a close examination: "There is not one clear instance of dependence upon Ezekiel until we come to Sirach,.... and in no composition earlier than Zech. 9–14 and the late portions of Joel is there even a balance of probability in favor of the priority of Ezekiel."

It would indeed be strange if priests, prophets, poets, and lawgivers had all turned to Ezekiel for inspiration and rested themselves on his work. He is not a writer whom we should expect to see often quoted. On the other hand, he is just the man to hold in memory and ponder the words of those by whom God "spoke in old time" (38:17). His own work was of course read and studied, but it came too late to leave in the Old Testament any considerable trace of its influence. It seems to me clear that Ps. 106:27 is taken verbally from Ezek. 20:23 (see above), though I agree with Burrows (p. 92) that the psalmist is also directly dependent here on Num. 14:28-35. In almost every case, however, in which the fact of borrowing can be surely demonstrated, it is evident that Ezekiel is the debtor. The instances in which he makes direct literary use of writings now generally acknowledged to be of late date are both very numerous and very conspicuous. Reference has already been made to his great indebtedness to the latest documents of the Pentateuch, and it is also certain that he was well acquainted with prophetical literature belonging to the Persian period.

The most important examples (in the present stage of Old Testament criticism) are those of his dependence on Second Isaiah. Burrows has treated the passages well, though his conclusion might perhaps have been stated more emphatically, in view of its significance. No one, I think, who has studied both books and is capable of weighing literary evidence can doubt that the long homily in Ezek. 34 is based ultimately on Is. 56:9-11,[34] in the same way that 31:3-18 and 32:17-32 are based on Is. 14:4-20. Ezek. 16:25 is a conscious exaggeration of Is. 57:7 f. (in the same poem), and it is hardly by accident that vs. 26 proceeds with the Egyptian alliance, precisely as vss. 8 f. continue in the older poem (see *The Second Isaiah*, pp. 109, 431 f.). The passage 18:7-9 seems to contain verbal reminiscences of Is. 58:7; Ezek. 23:33 f. borrows likewise from Is. 51:17; and 26:10 from Is. 60:6. In *The Second Isaiah*, p. 108, I have enumerated the chief items of evidence in Ezek. chaps. 20, 22, 34, 37, and 39 (very clear and striking examples). I repeat here one of these observations: "In 22:30 f. is expanded the very striking and original utterance, Is. 59:15 f.; 63:5."

The significance of Ezekiel's constant dependence on Jeremiah will be better understood when the fact is recognized, as ultimately it must be, that the book of Jer. was compiled in the middle of the third century, and that a very considerable part of its material was composed at about the time of the compilation. Some of the facts on which this assertion is based are presented and very briefly discussed in *The Second Isaiah*, pp. 95 ff., 99, and 107 f.

From all the preceding considerations, and especially from the linguistic features, it appears certain that the book of Ezekiel is a product

---

[34] So also are the two similar passages in Jeremiah, 12:9 f. (unquestionably!) and 23:1-4.

of the Greek period. There is still other evidence pointing definitely to the same conclusion.

I have argued elsewhere (*Marti Festschrift*, p. 284) that chap. 26 refers to the capture and destruction of Tyre by Alexander the Great. It was he who built the great mole from the mainland to the island-city, and over it drove his chariots into the streets (vss. 10 f.). The author of the prophecy shows his knowledge of ancient history; he is well aware that Nebuchadrezzar's siege of Tyre was fruitless (29:17–20).[35] From the strange position of the words "Nebuchadrezzar king of Babylon" in vs. 7 it is evident that they are a later addition to the text. The verse originally read as follows: "Thus saith the Lord God: Behold, I will bring upon Tyre *a king of kings*, from the north, with horses, chariots, and horsemen; with an assembly of many peoples" (observe the reading of the Greek version, and compare especially 38:4–7, 9, 15, where this same portentous invasion is again predicted!). The terrible warriors 'from the north' are the Macedonians, as in Habakkuk and Joel; the 'king of kings' is Alexander. Every feature of the description in the chapter, as well as the actual history of the siege and the complete destruction with which it ended, will be seen to bear out this interpretation.

Another very celebrated problem of the prophecy has this same solution. Who are the fearsome warriors coming in hordes from the north, depicted at such length in Chaps. 38 and 39; the most terrible invaders of all time, who "in the latter years" are destined to "come like a storm, like a cloud to cover the land," after the Israelites are again dwelling peacefully in Jerusalem and the surrounding country? They are similarly described in Jer. 4:13; 6:22 f.; and, under the figure of locusts, in the book of Joel. Two observations are certain, and to be emphasized, at the outset: *first*, that the memory of a mighty invasion lies behind all this description; and *second*, that the prophet passes over from the picture of actual happenings into the realm of eschatology, predicting the destruction of the terrible conqueror and his forces at the end of the present age; as Daniel passes over, in 11:40–45, from the actual history of the Seleucid king and his army to the prediction of his final downfall—a prophecy which indeed in its details was not fulfilled. It has been customary to say that Ezekiel alludes to a Scythian

---

[35] On the *date* in 29:17, see above, p. 62.

invasion, though the supposition is justified neither by any known history nor by the prophet's treatment. There certainly is here no allusion to the descent of a barbarian rabble, hardly touching Palestine at all, and effecting no important change in Western Asia. That which Ezekiel and his fellow prophets describe is the descent of highly trained and thoroughly equipped armies, such armies as never had been seen before, sweeping all before them and changing the face of the known world; invaders of such epoch-making importance that their destruction by Yahwè's special intervention is to be the great event making possible the dawn of the new age.

Who is "Gog, of the land of Magog, the prince of Rosh, Meshech, and Tubal," he who brought under his banner not only the peoples of the north, but also Persia (!), Egypt (concealed under the name "Put"? see Gen. 10:6),[36] Ethiopia, the inhabitants of the Ionian coastlands, and of the isles of the sea?

In the summer of 1928, a letter from Professor Nöldeke (then in his ninety-third year) informed me that he had again, after many years, undertaken and finished the task of reading through the book of Ezekiel in the Hebrew, with the help of the Greek version; and that he had become convinced that it is a work of very late date. Among the numerous interesting observations which he made, there was one which startled me: Gog, he remarked, is plainly Alexander the Great. This conclusion reached by the Nestor of living orientalists appears to me certain beyond question. I had myself paid little attention to Gog and Magog, and probably should not have made the discovery in any case.

As far as I am aware, this identification has been made but once in the past, namely by Winckler in his *Altorientalische Forschungen*, 2te Reihe, Band I (1898), pp. 160–171. His somewhat fantastic theory attracted little attention, and is now rarely mentioned. He held that

---

[36] Of course Egypt must have accompanied Put and Cush in Gog's mustering of the peoples. The avoidance of the name may be significant, since at the time when I suppose the book of Ezekiel to have been composed Egypt was the dominant power in Palestine, and the prophet might well have preferred not to predict openly the utter destruction of that nation among the others which were doomed (39:4). Elsewhere in the prophecy *old* Egypt, the Egypt of the Pharaohs, is promised a miserable fate; and it may be merely accidental that nothing is said which could be applied to the kingdom of the Ptolemies.

the Gog episode, chaps. 38 and 39, is a late interpolation in the book of Ezekiel, where it obviously is out of place, since in it the Jews are represented as having long since returned to Palestine from the exile. The Jewish editor made use of an old Babylonian myth, "the Götterdämmerung of the Babylonians," shaping it to his purpose, which was to picture the invasion and foretell the ultimate annihilation of the allconquering Greeks. Winckler's decision in favor of Alexander as the prototype of the Hebrew Gog was chiefly influenced by the very significant verse 39:6: "I will send a fire on Magog and on those who dwell securely in the isles (*'iyyīm*)."

The verse just quoted shows plainly enough where "the land of Magog" was conceived by this writer to be. The name is used by him (with Gen. 10:2 in mind) to designate *the Macedonian Kingdom*, to which the *'iyyīm* (the Grecian coastlands and islands) are joined. It is obvious that he could not have introduced "Javan" anywhere in these two chapters without spoiling his apocalyptic vision.[37] And the allusion to Alexander's invasion, with his conquest of Persia and Egypt as well as of the "northern" countries, is made as plain as it could be made in an apocalyptic vision with its essential mystery. The name *Gog* is simply abbreviated from *Magog* (so Nöldeke), and thus admirably serves its purpose.

The subject might be pursued much further to advantage, if space permitted. It may be queried whether, in the obscure repetition of chap. 38, the prophet foretells *both* the actual invasion and its fatal repetition at the end of the present age. It seems to be implied that Israel was not actually harmed by Gog himself (38:8, last clause), and it might well be said that the God of Israel was 'glorified in the eyes of the nations' (vs. 16) when Alexander spared Jerusalem. At all events, the problematic *wĕ-shōbabtīka* in 38:4 and 39:2, which Herrmann, pp. 245, 252 f., tries in vain to explain, means "I will bring thee back again," that is, for a second invasion. The allusion in 38:13 also deserves mention. Herrmann, p. 247, comments: "Was 13 soll, ist nicht

---

[37] This fact explains the problematic "Rōsh" in 38:2, 3 and 39:1. The three names, "Javan, Tubal, and Meshech," form a standing combination, familiar from Gen. 10:2 and 1 Chron. 1:5, and *repeated by the author of this prophecy* in 27:13. Here in 38 f. the triad appears as "Rōsh, Meshech, and Tubal." Javan was, beyond all comparison, the "chief" of the kingdoms.

recht einzusehen," and he inclines to pronounce it a gloss. But no better explanation could be asked than is furnished by the parallel in Joel 4:6-8, *addressed to the Phoenician merchants*: "The children of Judah and Jerusalem ye have sold *unto the sons of the Grecians*, that ye might remove them far from their border;. . . .and I will sell your sons and daughters into the hand of the children of Judah, and they shall sell them *to the men of Sheba*, to a nation far off." This was one of the incidental features of the conquest by the Grecian armies. "Sheba, and Dedan, and the merchants of Tarshish" were alert to make their profit.

It should be beyond all doubt that the "Northerner" whose ultimate fate is described, in apocalyptic style, in Joel 2:20, is the "Gog" of Ezekiel; and that his armies, which are given such frequent and impressive mention also in the book of Jeremiah (not only the passages cited above, but also 50:3, 9, 41 f.; 51:2, 14, 27) are the invaders of 332 B. C. To these prophecies are to be added, moreover, Habakkuk, Zech. 9:1-8 (cf. vs. 13), Is. 14:4-20, and 23:1-18.[38]

In general, the atmosphere of Ezekiel is manifestly that of Daniel, Joel, and the last chapters of Zechariah. As for the two last-named books, a very striking example of close relationship is afforded by the curious conception of *the river proceeding from the temple*, flowing eastward from Jerusalem and entering the Dead Sea; Ezek. 47:1-12. This same river appears also in Zech. 14:8 (half of the waters flowing toward the eastern sea, and half of them toward the western sea), and in Joel 4:18 b. Herrmann, pp. 294 f., in an excursus entitled "Der wunderbare Strom, der unter dem Tempel entspringt," has collected the passages referring to this 'river,' for it appears also in certain psalms, as well as in the New Testament. He remarks very truly that the passages in Joel and Zechariah are not dependent on Ezekiel. There is very good reason to hold, on the contrary, that the author of the book of Ezekiel, following his habit illustrated in so many other places, is here elaborating in his own fashion the idea provided by the other prophets. In any case, this apocalyptic notion is a property of the third century B. C.

As for Daniel: aside from the atmosphere of the apocalypse, and its

<hr/>

[38] See the article "Alexander the Great in the O. T. Prophecies," in the *Marti Festschrift* (1925), pp. 281-286.

characteristc features, in which the two writings are so closely related, there is in Ezek. 31:5 f.; 10, last clause; 12 b, 13, clear evidence of direct dependence on Dan. 4:7-14 (10-17). I have shown elsewhere (see below) that the first half of the book of Daniel, chaps. 1-6, was composed c. 245 B. C. But there is still plainer proof of the literary relation. In Ezek. 14:14, 20 Daniel is mentioned, between Noah and Job, as one of three foremost saints of Israel; and again, in 28:3, as the type of wisdom. These facts are ordinarily explained by saying that narratives about Daniel, and the story of Job, must have been familiar as early as the sixth (or rather, the seventh) century B. C., although in the literature known to us they appear much later. This explanation might be considered plausible, though certainly to be held under suspicion, if only *one* late book were thus to be given an ancient prototype; but the supposition of *two* such cases, on the basis of a single literary allusion, is too improbable to be seriously entertained. The plain fact is, that the widely read and widely quoting author of Ezekiel was familiar both with our book of Job and with the primitive form (chaps. 1-6) of the book of Daniel.

This enables us to determine approximately the date of Ezekiel. For the dating of the original form of Daniel, the book of popular stories, I may be permitted to quote from my article "Daniel" in the 14th ed. of the *Encyclopaedia Britannica*, p. 29: "The date is indicated with great probability by the allusions and the symbolism in chap. 2. The historical sketch terminates with the attempted alliance, through marriage, of the Ptolemaic and Seleucid kingdoms at a time when the contrast between the two was like that between iron and clay. This would perfectly apply to the political conditions at the time when the crushing blow was inflicted on the northern kingdom by Ptolemy III. Euergetes in 246 B. C., immediately after the murder of Antiochus II., the Seleucid king, and his newly espoused wife Berenice, the daughter of Ptolemy II. At no other time in the history of the two kingdoms was the contrast so strongly marked; the northern kingdom was not only impotent, it was actually crumbling. The provinces of the Euphrates and Tigris were now lost; Asia Minor was soon to follow; the two sons of Antiochus II. were arrayed against each other." The most probable date for Daniel 1-6 would seem to be very soon after 246 and presumably before 240, the year of the peace concluded between Ptolemy III. and Seleucus II.[39]

The lower limit for the date of Ezekiel is given by the fact that this prophet is mentioned, along with the Twelve, by Ben Sira, c. 180 B. C. It is of course necessary to suppose that the book had for some time been in existence, and that its author was already recognized in Jerusalem as one of the Hebrew prophets. A date c. 230 meets the conditions perfectly, allowing ample time in either direction, and agreeing with whatever is known as to the time when the collection of the Hebrew prophetical writings was definitely closed.

A date near the end of the third century satisfies the requirement of the language (!) of the book and of its use of other O. T. writings, and is also favored by every other consideration. The commentators, one and all, hear the sound of a degenerate age throughout the prophecy, and note the fact with emphasis. Ezekiel, they say, is distinctly one of the "Epigonen" in his mode of thought, religious ideas, and literary habits. And yet, according to the dating which these commentators never doubt, the priest Ezekiel, for many years resident in Jerusalem, had received his education in the great days of Josiah, while his own father presumably had seen the prophet Isaiah! But it is a true estimate, that his work bears the mark of 'the latter days.' The theophany which he describes is of the sort which we should expect to find in the book of Enoch, and the conventional circumlocution used in dealing with such subjects is also characteristic of that age. He sees "a likeness as of the appearance of a man," 1:26 b; "a likeness as the appearance of fire," 8:2; there appeared to him "as it were a sapphire stone as the appearance of the likeness of a throne," 10:1; and there are very many similar instances. The chariot of the cherubim seems to carry us a long way down from the days of Jehoiachin. I have read with appreciation the learned and interesting monograph by Dr. Lorenz Dürr, *Ezechiels Vision von der Erscheinung Gottes im Lichte der vorderasiatischen Altertumskunde*, but can find in it nothing to make plausible a Babylonian origin or an early date for Ezekiel's picture. The one close analogy is to be found in certain coins and low reliefs of the Ptolemaic

---

[39] The above conclusions, as well as those relating to the composition of the book of Daniel, I had already stated fully in 1909, in my *Notes on the Aramaic Part of Daniel* (Transactions Conn. Acad. of Arts and Sciences, XV, pp. 241-282).

period, in which winged creatures of composite form rest on a structure in which *wheels* are a conspicuous feature.

It has often been remarked as a curious fact that a priest transported to Babylonia and expecting the destruction of Jerusalem should have devoted so much space to the exact measurements (an astonishing list!), specifications, equipment, and even minor details of service, of an imaginary temple assigned to the remote future. But for a priest living in Jerusalem in the latter part of the third century, the construction of just such an elaborate plan as this would have been very natural indeed. Zerubbabel's temple, which never had been a magnificent building (Ezra 3:12), had stood for nearly 300 years and doubtless was in need of considerable repair, even if it was not felt to be out of date and inadequate. It would not be strange if the routine of its service, under changing conditions, should have departed in some respects from the prescriptions of the Pentateuch, with the full approval of its ministers, who felt that the new times permitted a certain amount of innovation. There must have been many who hoped for a new and more imposing edifice, especially since the temple on Mount Gerizim was still an unpleasant rival. To prepare the plan of such a building and its equipment, even before benefactor and architect were in sight, was as natural a proceeding as could be imagined. This, to all appearance, is what we may see in Ezek. 40–48, the 'Entwurf' of a Jerusalem priest, which he probably hoped might be made useful some day, even if not in his own time.

As for the preferment of the Zadokite priests, the impression given by the book of Ezekiel is that this was something new; perhaps merely hoped for, not yet realized. The late Dr. Kaufmann Kohler, in his *Origins of Synagogue and Church*, pp. 11 f., remarks significantly that it is otherwise only in very late sources that this especial prominence of the Zadokites appears. There certainly is no trace of it in the writings of the Chronicler; the nearest approach to it—if indeed it is an approach—is in 2 Chron. 31:10; but we may suppose that it arose soon after his day.

We now, perhaps, may conjecture the reason for the position which the book of Ezekiel occupies in the canon of Melito of Sardis, quoted in Eusebius, *Hist. Eccl.*, IV, 26; a treatment of the book which has attracted much attention, and generally has been regarded as a mere curiosity. Sardis, as we now know, had been the home of a Jewish colony for several centuries B. C., and doubtless had its line of Jewish scholars to the time of Melito and thereafter. The Jerusalem tradition, as we have seen, admitted no 'Ezekiel of Tell Abib' as the real author of this prophecy, but was content to accept the great book as it stood, while significantly discouraging any "higher criticism." It would seem that the Bishop of Sardis obtained his instruction as to the Hebrew canon from a truly authoritative source. In his list, after finishing with the poetical books of the Old Testament, he comes to the prophets, and writes: "Isaiah, Jeremiah. Of the Twelve Prophets, one book. Daniel, Ezekiel, Esdras."

VI

THE EDITOR'S WORK

The original 'Ezekiel,' as the preceding chapters have shown, was a pseudepigraph purporting to come from the reign of Manasseh, but in fact composed many centuries later. It was converted into a prophecy of the so-called 'Babylonian Golah' by an editor who accomplished his undertaking (in all probability) not many years after the original work had appeared. This redaction was not the result of any chance notion or caprice on the part of the man who effected the strange transformation; on the contrary, it was one of several features of a literary movement which seems to have originated in the middle of the third century B. C., having for its purpose the vindication of the religious tradition of Jerusalem.

For more than twenty years past I have been endeavoring to show—what at present seems to be recognized by comparatively few—that the breach between the Jews and the Samaritans, resulting in an enduring hostility which was especially bitter in the time between Alexander the Great and John Hyrcanus, brought about a most important turning point in the history of Palestine, and left a deep mark on the literature of the Old Testament. It was not a mere matter of petty jealousy, the result of a narrow spirit on the part of the Jewish people and their leaders and of insolent rivalry on the part of the Samaritans, but a truly internecine struggle in which it seemed at the outset that either side might win.[40]

The Samaritans claimed—had always claimed, with some good reason—that they were the true bearers of the old Israelite tradition, in opposition to the pretensions of Jerusalem and Judea. The partial destruction of the city and the burning of the temple by the Chaldeans, with the accompanying flight of the people for temporary refuge in the neighboring regions, furnished the adversary with a deadly weapon. *The all-important tradition was broken off*, finally and fatally. Who

---

[40] For a recent attempt to describe this "turning point" I would refer especially to my article "Sanballat the Horonite," in the *Journal of Biblical Literature*, Vol. XLVII (1928), pp. 380–389.

could tell to what extent the city was repopulated by the eager foreigners round about—Edomites, Ammonites, Phoenicians, Philistines, Arabs,—who thereupon had taken their part in the restoration of a contaminated service of Yahwè on the former site? They had the Pentateuch, indeed, but no longer the true succession of its ministers, which they on Mount Gerizim unquestionably possessed—and Shechem was by far the older sanctuary. There doubtless were many features of the elaborate service of the temple at Jerusalem, in the fourth century, which had no counterpart in the ritual of the Samaritans, and were asserted by the latter to be innovations and illegitimate. Where did they come from? Until this question could be satisfactorily answered, it is plain that the Jewish church was at a serious disadvantage.

If the Samaritans had also in their hands the exaggerated account of the destruction and depopulation of Jerusalem given in 2 Kings 25, it might seem to have added greatly to the ammunition at their disposal. In fact, however, its effect apparently adverse to the claims of the Jewish tradition was completely nullified by other documents; nay, more than this, there is very strong reason to conclude that this very picture of the utter abandonment of Jerusalem was designed by a Jewish apologist as one effective weapon of the arsenal against the Shechemites (see below).

The complete and final victory for Jerusalem was gained, not by any use or show of force, nor by any political turn of fortune, but by a very ingenious reconstruction of history. The genuine old tradition was preserved, entire and uncontaminated, by way of the deportation to Babylonia. All the best part of Israel was carried away by the Chaldeans, remained intact and unmixed with foreign elements in the land of exile, and eventually returned in triumph to the completely deserted cities, Jerusalem and the cities of Judea, to restore everything just as it had existed in former time.

In regard to the numbers of the successive deportations, there is a very significant difference between the statements in Jer. 52:28–30 and those in 2 Kings. According to the former (which unquestionably is the more deserving of credence), the total was but a small fraction of the population. The account in 2 Kings 24 f., which as it stands is thoroughly self-contradictory and impossible, has probably been altered, with a purpose, from its original form.[41] In 24:14 we hear of "10,000 captives" in the time of Jehoiachin, with the added statement that "none remained save the poorest sort of the people of the land." In 25:11 f. (eleven years later) we read that "the residue of the people that were left in the city,....and the residue of the multitude" were carried away captive by Nebuzaradan, who however "left of the poorest of the land to be vinedressers and husbandmen." Thus Jerusalem was completely abandoned, and the Babylonian *golah* greatly increased, at the end of Zedekiah's reign. As for "the people that were left in Judea" (vs. 22), they all, "both small and great" (vs. 26), fled to Egypt after the assassination of Gedaliah. Both Jerusalem and the cities of Judah were left utterly without inhabitant, *and remained thus until the return of the exiles* (this certainly is the intention of the account). The land had a sabbath rest for "seventy" years (2 Chron. 36:21).[42]

The account of the Restoration is well thought out in its details. Indeed, when the Jewish apologists once became convinced that there must have been such a restoration, the details came naturally. There is complete authentication, and official authorization by the Persian kings, in the successive periods. Cyrus and the first Return, with provision for the worship at Jerusalem and the support of the priests and Levites (the greater part of this edict of Cyrus now preserved only in First Esdras; see *Ezra Studies*, pp. 116–135, and the references given in my articles "Third Book of Ezra" and "Ezra and Nehemiah, Books" in the 14th ed. of the *Encycl. Britannica*); Darius and the temple, based on Haggai and Zechariah, though the mistaken chronology then current made it Darius II.; Artaxerxes (II.) and the Law, with the indispensable 'Ezra'; Nehemiah and the complete purification of the Israelite blood ("I cleansed them from *all* strangers," Neh. 13:30, completing what Ezra had begun); and—perhaps most important of all—the Great

[41] It nevertheless has been reproduced in Jer. 52, where it flatly contradicts the statements made in the three verses above mentioned.

[42] Another item in which the narrative of 2 Kings 24 f. seems to have been altered in the interest of the later theory is that of the vessels of the temple service. According to 24:13, "all the vessels of gold" were cut in pieces and carried off as bullion—a most natural proceeding. But for the complete restoration these vessels were needed. The editor does not, of course, remove the former statement, but expressly contradicts it in 25:15. The correction is made more emphatically in 2 Chron. 36; the vessels were carried (intact) to Babylonia in the times of Jehoiakim (vs. 7), Jehoiachin (vs. 10), and Zedekiah (vs. 18).

List, authenticated by the Persian governor Sheshbazzar in 538 (Ezra 2:63), and again—the same list—by Nehemiah, who found it in the year 384 (see *The Second Isaiah*, pp. 458 ff.) and made it the basis of his great census (Neh. 7:5).

The true "Israel," the priests, the Levites (in their more precise divisions: Levites, singers, porters), and even the temple-servants called Nethinim, all were restored exactly as (according to the Chronicler) they had been in the days of David and Solomon. The many lists of 1 and 2 Chron., in their correspondence with the Great List, which presumably was compiled from a census of the third century, proved this completely. All these elements of the renovated Hebrew community had only to return from Babylonia and reoccupy "their" cities, which had remained without inhabitant for more than a generation! Three hundred years after the destruction of Jerusalem all this could be asserted without danger of successful contradiction; no one could prove the contrary.

That this is merely a brilliant theory, lacking any basis of fact, is certain. It left the Samaritans no standing ground, and ultimately became the accepted view of Israelite history in the Persian period; and yet it is very interesting to see how slowly it gained general recognition in Jerusalem, after its first promulgation in the middle of the third century. The great Return, rivalling in importance the rescue from Egypt, receives no mention even in the Psalter, with the single exception of the picturesquely imaginative Ps. 137. Even Ben Sira, in his résumé of the heroes and triumphs of Israel, has not a word to say in regard to the restoration, though he must have been acquainted with the legend. I shall show that the author of the original prophecy of Ezekiel not only makes no allusion to the Babylonian Golah, but also expresses himself repeatedly in a manner which would hardly have been possible if he had been persuaded of the existence of this particular body of exiles. The late book of Jeremiah, only very slightly earlier than Ezekiel, contains some passages which seem to show knowledge either of the completely formulated hypothesis or else of its preliminary stage. Chapters 24 and 27–29 are very obviously a product of the school to which the Chronicler belonged,[43] and the mysteriously inter-

[43] The correspondence described and recorded in chap. 29 stands on no higher plane, in point of historical value, than the "Epistle of Jeremiah" in the Apocrypha.

jected passages in chaps. 50 and 51 (50:8, 28, 33; 51:6, 45, 50) make
the same impression.

As for the original Ezekiel, the lack of any reference to exiles in
Babylonia, even where such reference is made most natural by the
context, seems to show that this author was either unacquainted with
the new theory of the Babylonian Golah or else felt no interest in it.
He knows of "captives" who are "scattered through the countries,"
6:8 f.; 11:16 f.; 12:15 f.; 20:41; 28:25; 34:6, 12 f., 27; 36:19 ff., 24;
37:21; 38:8; 39:27 f.; and the return to Palestine is invariably "from
all the nations and lands." The passage 34:27, "They shall know that
I am the Lord, when I have broken the bars of their yoke, and have
delivered them out of the hand of those who have made bondmen of
them," shows that the figure of captivity and bondage is taken from
the servitude of the fathers in Egypt; and that this prophet (like the
Hebrew prophets in general) refers to the Dispersion whenever he
speaks of exiles. If he had credited the account of the restoration from
Babylonia, or even supposed that that land contained an especially
important nucleus of the Israelite people, it is incredible that he should
have made no allusion to this incomparable 'remnant' at any point in
these thirty-nine chapters. If he wrote at about the year 230, it is not
strange that he should have been untouched by the recent reconstruction of Jewish history.

The author of the Books of Chronicles, at all events, was convinced
of the essential truth of the theory. His whole great work was composed in order to establish the fact of the Restoration, and to delimit
the true and uncontaminated Palestinian "Israel" with its authenticated clans and families, and with its ancient and highly specialized
temple-service distinguishing it from any other Hebrew religious community. Every detail in his book, from the very beginning, contributes
to this purpose. He shuts out, effectually, the Samaritans and their
tradition, picturing 'those of the return' as fanatically exclusive
legalists, content with their narrow view of the world and able to keep
clear of outsiders. His 'history' won the day for Judah and Jerusalem.
More than this, it became the textbook of Jewish origins for all the
world; its veracity, as regards the Persian period, hardly questioned to
the present day. In particular, the theory of the development of
Hebrew and Jewish literature and institutions which has prevailed

since the latter part of the nineteenth century, and is commonly associated with the name of Wellhausen, rests chiefly on the Chronicler's achievement. It centers in the work of 'Ezra', and builds its own peculiar framework on the account of Jerusalem and 'the exiles' created by the late and utterly untrustworthy Jewish apologist.

The Chronicler's work was not the only available weapon of attack and defence. There was need of something more than the authority of a single book, and the need was supplied. As I have demonstrated in my *Second Isaiah*, the ingeniously conceived interpolations in Is. 43:14; 44:28; 45:1, 48:14, 20 (one entire verse, but otherwise only single words) created an 'exilic' prophecy and gave most important support to the fiction of the restoration of Jerusalem by the command of Cyrus. I have also attempted to show that *the forming of a sacred library* was another feature of the literary movement in Jerusalem, in the third century B. C., in defence of the Jewish church and vindication of its authority as the unique repository of a divine literary tradition. See the section entitled "The Library of Israel's Prophets" in *The Second Isaiah*, pp. 94–98, especially pp. 97 f. But there was another undertaking, more directly effective, similar to that which was accomplished in the case of Second Isaiah and probably contemporary with it, namely the refashioning of the great prophecy now known as the book of Ezekiel.

After the belief in the return from the Babylonian exile was once fully established, there were several considerations which rendered it very natural to see in this work a possible 'exilic' prophecy. The conditions in Judea are those described in 2 Kings 24 and 25. The events of Zedekiah's reign, especially, are in the foreground; Jehoiakim and Jehoiachin have already passed off the scene (chap. 19). The destruction of the city by the Chaldeans is imminent, close at hand. Yet the prophet *knows nothing about Jeremiah* (see Chapter IV, at the end). He therefore cannot have lived in Jerusalem in the days of Zedekiah. He speaks of a wholesale dispersion from the holy land, already in process, and repeatedly promises a return "from all the nations and countries." *The true Israel* was preserved only in Babylonia (so the Chronicler had demonstrated), yet the prophet makes no allusion to that particular *golah*. This could be explained on the supposition that he himself lived there. The manner in which the seer, in the prophecy, is carried about by the spirit from place to place gave the final suggestion. In chapters 8 f., at all events, he is actually in Jerusalem. It was only necessary to make it plain, by express statement, that he was miraculously transported to and from the holy land.

In order to turn the oracle of Manasseh's reign into an utterance from the Babylonian captivity little change was necessary. A few explanatory and supplementary additions were indispensable; and, in rare instances, it must be shown by the slight change in the form of plural suffixed pronouns that the prophet's hearers are at a distance, not directly addressed. The dates, one and all, required revision, always with the least possible alteration. In only one passage, 12:10 ff., was any such change as transposition of words required. Nothing, of course, was to be *omitted*; to this principle the redactors of the Hebrew sacred writings always adhered as strictly as possible.[44]

I subjoin a list of the editorial changes, following the order of the successive chapters. I certainly make no claim that the list is final; others may improve upon it; but the analysis is in almost every case quite obvious. The additions and alterations made by the redactor (RB) are printed in bold-face type. The translation is generally that of the English Revised Version.

1:1–4. It came to pass in the thirtieth year, in the fourth month, in the fifth day of the month, **as I was among the captives by the river Chebar**, that the heavens were opened, and I saw visions of God. **In the fifth day of the month, which was the fifth year of King Jehoiachin's captivity, the word of God came expressly unto Ezekiel the priest, the son of Buzi, in the land of the Chaldeans by the river Chebar; and the hand of the Lord was there upon him.**[45] And I looked, and behold, a stormy wind came out of the north, etc.

3:11. And go, get thee **to them of the captivity** unto the children of thy people, and speak unto them.

---

[44] It was of course quite another matter when popular narratives, like those in Daniel, Tobit, Judith, etc., were freely reproduced from memory in various languages. Also, in combining documents which say nearly or quite the same thing it would seem permissible, and in some cases quite necessary, to omit a superfluous phrase or sentence; but even here the oriental editor always prefers, if possible, to let the parallel or even contradictory versions stand side by side.

[45] Possibly the last clause of vs. 3 formed a part of the original text, reading: "and the hand of the Lord was upon me."

3:14–16. So the spirit lifted me up, and took me away; and I went in bitterness, in the heat of my spirit, and the hand of the Lord was strong upon me. **And I came to them of the captivity at Tell Abib, that dwelt by the river Chebar, where they were dwelling, and I sat there appalled among them seven days. And it came to pass at the end of seven days**—And the word of the Lord came to me, saying, Son of man, I have made thee a watchman unto the house of Israel.

3:23. Then I arose, and went forth to the valley; and behold, the glory of the Lord stood there; **like the glory which I saw by the river Chebar;** and I fell on my face.

8:1. And it came to pass **in the sixth year,** in the fifth month, in the fifth day of the month, etc. (Regarding this date, and those which occur in the subsequent chapters, see the discussion in Chapter IV.)

8:3. **And he put forth the form of a hand, and took me by a lock of the hair of my head,** And the spirit lifted me up **between the earth and the heaven** and brought me **in the visions of God to Jerusalem** to the door of the gate of the inner court.

10:15. And the cherubim mounted up; **this is the living creature that I saw by the river Chebar;** and when the cherubim went, the wheels went beside them.

10:20. **This is the living creature that I saw under the God of Israel by the river Chebar;** and I knew that they were cherubim.

10:22. And as for the likeness of their faces, **they were the faces which I saw by the river Chebar, their appearances and themselves,** they went every one straight forward.

11:24f. And the spirit lifted me up and brought me, **to Chaldea, to the Golah,** in the vision, by the spirit of God; and the vision which I had seen went up from me. **And I spoke unto them of the captivity all the things that the Lord had shown me.**

12:10–12. This is the passage mentioned above as having given unusual trouble to the redactor. Indeed, the whole chapter opposed very manifest obstacles to his purpose. The translation of the passage in its original form has already been given, p. 41; the restored text reads as follows:

אמר אליהם אֶל כל בית ישראל אשר אתה בתוכם: אמר אני מופתכם כאשר עשיתי כן יעשה לכם בגולה בשבי תלכו: כה אמר אדוני יהוה הנשא המשא הזה בירושלים הנשיא אשר בתוככם על כתף ישא וגו'.

The overlined letters and words indicate the points at which the redactor was obliged to make his alterations. It is obvious that the address to the people which begins with "I am *your* sign" must be finished by saying, "as I have done, so shall be done *to you.*" But the second person plural could not possibly be permitted to stand in vs. 11 b! "Into exile, into captivity, *ye* shall go" could not be said to the Babylonian exiles. The clause beginning "Thus saith the Lord" was transposed to follow immediately upon the words "Say to them" in order to permit the use of the third person plural. With the restored reading, "in the midst of whom *thou art,*" at the end of vs. 10, compare vs. 2 a (!) and also vs. 19. Even after the redactor had made these changes, the Tell Abib setting could hardly seem plausible, especially since the scene of chap. 11 is Jerusalem, and (to say nothing of the first words of 12:19!) chap. 13 is also addressed directly to the people of Jerusalem and Judea. This passage, 12:10–12, is hardly less significant than 1:2 f. in the evidence which it affords of manipulation of the original text in order to effect the transfer from Jerusalem to Babylonia.

12:19. And say unto the people of the land, Thus saith the Lord God concerning the inhabitants of Jerusalem, upon the land of Israel, Ye **(they)** shall eat your **(their)** bread with carefulness, and ye **(they)** shall drink your **(their)** water with astonishment, that your **(her)** land may be desolate from all that is therein, because of the violence of all them that dwell therein.

13:9. And my hand shall be against the prophets that see vanity and divine lies; they shall not be in the council of my people, ... **nor shall they come to the land of Israel.**

19:9. The interpolated clause, **and they brought him to the king of Babylon** (recognized also by Bertholet as an interpolation), may or may not be the work of RB.

20:1. It came to pass **in the seventh year,** in the fifth month, the tenth day of the month, etc.

24:1f. The word of the Lord came to me **in the ninth year,** in the tenth month, in the tenth day of the month, saying, Son of man, **write thee the name of the day, even of this selfsame day: the king of Babylon drew close unto Jerusalem this selfsame day. And** utter a parable unto the rebellious house, etc.

24:21. And your sons and daughters **whom ye have left behind** shall fall by the sword.

24:24–27. And I shall be **(Ezekiel shall be)** unto you a sign; according to all that I have done **(he hath done)** shall ye do, when this cometh to pass. **And ye shall know that I am the Lord God. And thou, son of man, shall it not** be in the day when I take from them their strength, the joy of their glory, the desire of their eyes, and that whereupon they set their heart, their sons and daughters, that in that day he that escapeth shall come unto thee, to cause thee to hear it with thine ears? In that day shall thy mouth be opened to him which is escaped, and thou shalt speak, and be no more dumb, so shalt thou be a sign unto them; and they shall know that I am the Lord.

Verse 24 (along with 1:3) shows that for the name of the prophet we are indebted to the editor RB; the original work was anonymous. As for vss. 25–27, Hölscher, *Hesekiel*, p. 131, had already shown, for convincing reasons, that the passage is interpolated.

26:1. It came to pass **in the ninth year,** in the eleventh month, in the first day of the month, etc.

26:7. Behold, I will bring upon Tyre **Nebuchadrezzar king of Babylon** a king of kings from the north, etc.

29:1. **In the tenth year,** in the twelfth month, in the twelfth day of the month, the word of the Lord came unto me, etc.

29:17. And it came to pass in the thirty-first year **(the twenty-seventh year),** in the first month, in the first day of the month, etc.

30:20. It came to pass **in the eleventh year,** in the first month, in the seventh day of the month, etc.

31:1. It came to pass **in the eleventh year,** in the third month, in the first day of the month, etc.

32:1. It came to pass **in the eleventh year,** in the twelfth month, in the first day of the month, etc.

32:17. It came to pass in the thirty-second year **(the twelfth year),** in the first month, in the fifteenth day of the month, etc.

33:21 f. And it came to pass **in the twelfth year,** in the tenth month, in the fifth day of the month, **of our captivity, that one that had escaped out of Jerusalem came unto me, saying, The city is smitten. Now the hand of the Lord had been upon me in the evening, before he that had escaped came; and he had opened my mouth, until he came to me in the morning; and my mouth was opened, and I was no more dumb. And there came** that there came to me the word of the Lord, etc.

33:24, 27. Son of man, they that inhabit **these waste places in** the land of Israel say, etc. (cf. 7:2, 7).

As I live, surely they that are in the cities **(the waste places)** shall fall by the sword, and him that is in the open field will I give to the beasts to be devoured, and they that be in the strong holds and in the caves shall die of the pestilence.

It might be urged, in defence of the traditional text, that the prophet is here looking into the more distant future, as in the chapters which immediately follow. This, however, is forbidden by vss. 28 f. and 33. As was remarked in Chapter II (and is so plain as to need no remark), the latter part of the chapter shows that the prophet is *not* looking into the time subsequent to the fall of the city, but is warning of that event. He is not speaking of "waste places" caused by peaceful emigration from Palestine, but of devastation by the Chaldean armies (see vs. 27!); and the destruction of Jerusalem *has not yet taken place*, it is "coming" (vs. 33). With chaps. 34–37 the tone of the prophecy changes, and the subject in the foreground is the calamity of the great Dispersion, and the comforting promise of a general return to the holy land "from all the countries," conceived in somewhat the same way as in Second Isaiah. It is this change of subject, obviously, that led RB to insert in chap. 33 his episode of the 'fugitive.' It could not come later, and the precise place of its insertion was determined by the *date* in vs. 21 (RB created no date entire), which, with the aid of the retouching in vss. 24 and 27, could be made to carry the episode, vss. 21 f. Omit, therefore, the three words in vs. 24; and read *bè-ʿarīm*, instead of *bè-kharabōth*, in vs. 27.

40:1 f. In the thirty-fifth year (**the twenty-fifth year of our captivity**), in the beginning of the year, in the tenth day of the month, **in the fourteenth year after that the city was smitten, in the selfsame day** the hand of the Lord was upon me, and he brought me **thither; in the visions of God**[46] **he brought me to the land of Israel,** and set me down upon a very high mountain, etc.

When the foregoing editorial alterations are removed, the book is substantially as it left the hand of its author. The text has been badly preserved, it is true, but the corruption is by no means as extensive as some scholars have supposed. The chapters, and single paragraphs, are all in their original order, and there is no evidence of any editorial labors aside from those of RB. The great work, in its true form and character, is far more valuable for our understanding of the development of Hebrew literature and religion than the utterly anomalous and self-contradictory 'exilic' prophecy, out of place, as it stood, in any normal construction of Old Testament history.

The author of the prophecy, apparently a man of priestly rank resid-

---

[46] Observe the similar use of the same phrase in the interpolated portion of 8:3.

ing in Jerusalem, wished to set before his people, in full detail and with every variety of emphasis, the lesson to be learned from the past, in order that they might be aroused from their present condition of sin and indifference. He had at hand the best possible material for his purpose, in the record of the unexampled wickedness of the Southern Kingdom in the time of Manasseh, and the terrible calamity that had befallen the people, in their dispersion from the home land and especially in the devastation wrought by the armies of Nebuchadrezzar. What he especially wished to show was *that the people had been fully and definitely warned;* the punishment was not brought upon them until after they had heard the word of God uttered in sharp rebuke and with assurance of what was in store for them unless they should repent and mend their ways. At that very time "the Lord spoke by his servants the prophets" (2 Kings 21:10). The author of the book of Ezekiel set himself to imagine what some one of those prophets would have said—what must indeed have been their message—in describing the sin of the people and predicting the woes that were impending. The inspired prophets were given definite knowledge of future events; so believed the people of this later day in which Hebrew prophecy was looked upon as a thing of the past. This nameless prophet accordingly is made to foresee coming events in the same way in which other writers pictured Daniel.

Such imagining and recording of what "must have been" said and done is a perfectly legitimate and effective device, a well recognized branch of Hebrew literature, early and late. The Old Testament is greatly enriched by those rather numerous products of a fervent imagination which adopt the setting of an earlier age, returning to some critical period in the past history and putting the desired teaching into the mouth of some known or unknown spokesman of the desired truth. To this class of writings belong Deuteronomy, large portions of Jeremiah and Zechariah, Jonah, Daniel, Qoheleth—to mention no others, and to say nothing of the extra-canonical pseudepigrapha, some of them works of very great religious value. The words of Driver, *Introduction*, p. 85, in regard to the book of Deuteronomy are equally true as applied to our prophecy: "There is nothing implying an interested or dishonest motive on the part of the author; and this being so, its moral and spiritual greatness remains unimpaired."

INDEX

I. Names and Subjects

II. Passages